LETTERS FROM A SUFI TEACHER

BEING AN ABRIDGED TRANSLATION OF THE CELEBRATED "MAKTUBAT-E-SADI" OR THE COLLECTION OF ONE HUNDRED LETTERS COVERING DIFFERENT TOPICS OF SPIRITUAL TRAINING.

WRITTEN BY ONE OF THE EMINENT SUFIS OF THE SUB-CONTINENT

Sheikh Sharaf-ud-din Yahya Maneri

Translated by

Baijnath Singh

KITAB BHAVAN

New Delhi-110002 (India)

Kitab Bhavan
Publishers, Distributors, Exporters & Importers
1784, Kalan Mahal, Darya Ganj
New Delhi-110002 (India)

Phone : (91-11) 23277392/93, 23274686, 30906494
website : www.kitabbhavan.com
Email : nasri@vsnl.com
Fax : (91-11) 23263383

Edition 2005

Laser Typesetting at
Laser Track
Kalan Mahal, New Delhi-2

Published in India by:
Nusrat Ali Nasri for Kitab Bhavan
1784, Kalan Mahal, Darya Ganj
New Delhi-110002 [India]

Printed in India at:
Nice Printing Press
Khureji Khas, Delhi-110051

CONTENTS

FOREWORD

Shaikh Sharaf-ud-dîn was the son of Shaikh Yahyã. His birth place is Maneri, a village near Patnã in Bihãr (India). A love of knowledge and the religious life, and signs of spiritual greatness, were found in him from his early childhood. A strange Being was once seen by the cradle of the baby. The mother, frightened, reported the matter to her father, Shahãb-ud-dîn, a great saint. The latter consoled her, saying that the mysterious Presence was no less a Being than the Prophet Khezar[1] Himself, and that the baby was expected to be a man of great spiritual advancement. He acquired secular knowledge under Ashraf-ud-din, a famous professor of those days. He first refused to marry, but had to yield when, being ill, he was advised by the physician to take to marriage as the remedy for his disease. He left home after the birth of a son, travelled in many places, and was at last initiated (at, or near Delhi) by Najib-ud-dîn Firdausî. The latter made him his deputy on earth under a deed drawn twelve years earlier under the direction of the Prophet of Islãm Himself, asked him to leave the place, and quitted his body shortly after.

On his initiation, Sharaf-ud-dîn lived for many a long year in the woods of Bihiã and the Rãjgiri Hills. In his later days he adopted Bihãr (now a subdivisional town) as his residence, at the request of some of his friends and disciples. He died on Thursday, the 6th of Shawwãl, 782 Hijra, in the opening years of the 15th Century A.D. His titular name is Makhdûm-ul-Mulk, 'Master of the Kingdom or the World'. He was equally proficient in secular learning and esoteric

---

1. A mysterious Personage, according to some, a Prophet; according to others, a *Walî* or 'Friend of God'. He is supposed to be an Immortal Being, an invisible Teacher and Helper of Mankind. Moses was sent by God to seek His instruction. '*Khezar*' literally means 'green', a metaphorical expression for auspiciousness, blessedness, wholesomeness and fertility.

Knowledge, and possessed superhuman powers. His tomb at Bihãr is still resorted to as a place of sanctity by a large number of devout Mahommedans. He wrote many works, of which three only have yet been published. These are:—

(1) *Maktûbãt-i-Sadî*, a 'Series of a Hundred Letters' (or rather essays on definite subjects) addressed to his disciple Qãzî Shams-ud-dîn in 747 Hijra.

(2) *Maktûbãt-i-Bist-o-hasht*, a 'Series of 28 Letters', being replies to the correspondence of his senior disciple, Mozaffar, the prince of Balkh.

(3) *Fawãed-i-Ruknî*, a number of brief Notes prepared for the use of his disciple Rukn-ud-dîn.

The present booklet consists of the translation of copious extracts from *Maktûbãt-i-Sadî*, the most elaborate and comprehensive of the three published works, with Notes occasionally added from the other two with a view to elucidate or complete the subject in hand. These extracts, it is hoped, will cover the greater part of, if not all, the *principles* inculcated in these books, and are expected to give the reader a fair knowledge of the *Teaching* of the Author *in all its phases*. Matters relating to mere exoteric rites, legends and traditions have been omitted. The translation does not pretend to be always very literal, but an honest attempt has been made to present a faithful rendering of the original to the English-knowing public, that they may be able to better appreciate the Teachings of Islãm, and that the Brotherhood of Creeds may have one more advocate to plead its cause before the tribunal of the human intellect.

Gaya, (Bihãr)

BAIJNÃTH SINGH

LETTERS FROM A SÛFÎ TEACHER

ON MONOTHEISM (TAUHÎD)

Masters of the Path have divided monotheism into four stages. The first stage consists in repeating, vocally, without any inner conviction, "There is no God save Allãh."[1] This is hypocrisy, and does not profit on the day of resurrection. The second stage consists in repeating the said *logion* vocally with an inner conviction based upon conventional imitation (as in the case of ordinary people), or some form of reasoning (as in the case of an intellectual theist). This is verily the visible body of monotheism, frees one from gross polytheism and from hell, and leads to heaven. This second stage, though safer than the first, and less unstable, is for all that a low one, fit for old women.[2] The third stage consists in Light shining in the heart, which reveals the One Agent alone as the root of all phenomena, and the non-agency of all else. This is quite unlike the conviction of ordinary people or that of an intellectual theist. Such a conviction is a fetter to the soul, whereas the vision of the Light breaks all fetters. There must be difference between one who believes a certain gentleman to be in his house, on the testimony of others (as in the case of ordinary people), another who infers the residence of that gentleman in the house, because he sees his horses and servants at the gate (as in the case of the intellectual theist), and another who actually sees the gentleman in the house (as in the case of the third stage). In the third stage one sees the creatures and the Creator, and distinguishes them from Him. This much of separation still persists—hence it is not perfect union in the eyes of the Masters.

1. *Lã elãha ill' Allãh.*
2. Weak souls.—*Trans.*

The fourth stage consists in the pouring forth of the Divine Light so profusely, that it absorbs all individual existences in the eyes of the pilgrim. As in the case of the absorption of particles floating in the atmosphere in the light of the sun, the particles become invisible—they do not cease to exist, nor do they become the sun, but they are inevitably lost to sight in the overpowering glare of the sun—so, here, a creature does not become God, nor does it cease to exist. Ceasing to exist is one thing, invisibility is another... When thou lookest through a mirror, thou dost not see the mirror, for thou mergest in into the reflexion of thy face, and yet thou canst not say that the mirror has ceased to exist, or that it has become that reflexion, or that the reflexion has become the mirror. Such is the vision of the Divine Energy in all beings without distinction. This stage is called by the Sûfîs, absorption in monotheism. Many have lost their balance here: no one can pass through this forest without the help of the Divine Grace and the guidance of a Teacher, perfect, open-eyed, experienced in the elevations and depressions of the Path and inured to its blessings and sufferings... Some pilgrims attain to this lofty state only for an hour a week, some for an hour a day, some for two hours a day, some remain absorbed for the greater portion of their time....

Beyond the four is the stage of complete absorption, *i.e.*, losing the very consciousness of being absorbed and of seeking after God—for such a consciousness still implies separation. Here, the soul merges itself and the universe into the Divine Light, and loses the consciousness of merging as well. "Merge into Him, this is monotheism: lose the sense of merging, this is unity." Here there are neither formulae nor ceremonies, neither being nor non-being, neither description nor allusion, neither heaven nor earth. It is this stage alone that unveils the mystery: "All are non-existent save Him;" "All things are perishable save His Face;" "I am the True and the

Holy One." Absolute unity without duality is realised here. "Do not be deluded, but know: everyone who merges in God is not God."

The first stage of monotheism is like the outermost shell of the almond; the second stage is like the second shell; the third stage is like the core; the fourth stage is like the essence of the core—the oil of the almond. All these are known by the name of the almond, but each differs immensely from the others in status, result, and use.

This note should be studied patiently and intelligently, since it deals with the basis of all developments, activities, and supersensuous phenomena. It will explain the phraseology and the allusions in the writings of the saints, and throw light on the verses on monotheism and the stages thereof.

O brother! though an ant, thou mayest turn out to be a Solomon. Do not think thou art an impure sinner: though a gnat, thou mayest become a lion. God raises the monotheist out of the dualist, the faithful out of the faithless, and the devotee out of the sinner—*Letter 1.*

[The following extracts on monotheism from "The Series of 28 Letters," another work of the author, may be aptly added—*Trs.*]

According to a tradition of the Prophet, all beings were created out of Darkness, but each took in Light according to its capacity, and thus became luminous. Hence all beings are sparks of the Divine Light, and their luminosity is derived from It. Now one can fully understand the sacred verse: "God is the Light of heaven and earth"—*Letter* 17.

Thou-ness and I-ness pertain to our world. They do not exist in the region of the Beloved. He is the one Reality: futile is the assertion of any existence but His—*Letter 2.*

TURNING TO GOD OR CONVERSION (TAUBÃH)

Taubãh literally means to turn back. But the nature of the turning must be different with different individuals according to the difference in their conditions and stages. Ordinary people would turn from sin with apology in order to escape punishment; middling ones would turn from their deeds to secure the regard of the Master; the Elect would turn from all worlds, here and hereafter, and feel the insignificance and non-existence thereof in order to realise the glory of the Maker. The turning of a beginner cannot be permanent. A saint says of himself; "I turned back 70 times and failed each time; but my seventy-first turning proved steady, and I failed no more."

Khwãja (Master) Zoonoon of Egypt observes that the Taubãh or ordinary people consists in turning from sins, that of the Elect in turning from heedlessness.

Khwãja Sobaid and many others are of opinion that Taubãh consists in remembering one's past transgressions and being ever ashamed of them, so that one may not grow proud of one's many virtues. On the other hand, Khwãja Junnaid and many others hold the view that Taubãh consists in forgetting past transgressions, *i.e.*, in expunging their impressions from the heart, so that it may become as pure as if it had never committed them.

Taubãh is obligatory for all pilgrims at all times, since for each pilgrim there is always a stage higher than his present one. If he halts at any stage, he stops his pilgrimage and commits sin.

Taubãh consists in a firm and sincere resolution to abstain from sins, so as to assure God of one's unwillingness to commit them in future; and in compensating, to one's best ability, those one has harmed in any way.....

Taubãh is the basis of all developments, as the ground is for the foundation of a building. The chief requisite is Imãn (peace, faith, or moral sense). Taubãh and Imãn appear together, and the latter illumines the heart in proportion to the former.

The real Taubãh lies in turning from one's nature. When the disciple turns from his nature he becomes another; *i.e.*, he does not become another man, but his qualities change. Then he unfolds true Imãn, which sweeps away many-ness and leads to unity. Ere the turning, Imãn is but conventional and nominal. "How long will you worship God with your tongue only? This is no better than worshipping desires. So long as thou dost not become a Muslim from *within*, how canst thou be a Muslim merely from *without*?" The lame ass of conventional faith and the lip-behaviour that we have cannot help us to tread the Path.

None ought to despair under any circumstance whatsoever. Here work is without a motive, and requires no payment. Many are instantly raised from the level of image-worship to a stage higher than the angels and heaven. The Lord does whatever He wishes. "How" and "why" find no room here. May God make thee a seer of His, and remove thee from thyself! Do thou aspire high, though thou art low at present. O brother, human aspiration should stoop to nothing, either on earth or in heaven! "Such men are so constituted as to care for neither hell nor heaven. They seek God and God only, and spurn what is not He."

Theosophy (Tasavvuf) is ceaseless motion, since standing water becomes stagnant. A man may corporeally be in his closet, yet his spirit may run to the Malakût[1] and the Jabrût.[2] Rapid motion, like the morning breeze, can neither be seen not grasped—*Letters 2-4*.

---

1. The astral and lower mental planes.
2. The higher mental plane.

ON SEEKING THE TEACHER

The Saints on the Path—blessed be they—unanimously declare that it is incumbent upon a neophyte, after the maturity of his conversion (Taubãh), to seek a Teacher, perfect, experienced in the elevations and depressions of the Path, its joys and sorrows, possessed of balance, and versed in the internal ailments of a disciple and their remedies.....

Though in the beginning one does not need a Teacher, and the seed can be sown merely with the help of Divine Grace, the seed, when sown in the soil of the heart, does need a Teacher for its further growth, for the following reasons given in the books of the saints:

1. Since one cannot go to the Kãbã[1] without a guide, albeit the way is visible and sensuous, and the pilgrim possesses eyes and feet, it is impossible without a guide to tread the occult Path trodden by 120,000 prophets, which has no visible track and is supersensuous.

2. As there are many thieves and robbers on a sensuous way, and one cannot travel without a guide, so on the occult Path there are many robbers in the guise of the world, the desire-nature and the elementals, and one cannot travel without the guidance of a Master.

3. There are many precipices and dangers on the Path, leading to one or other of the many heretic schools formed by those who, having entered the Path without a Perfect Guide, on the strength of their own intellectual resources, fell and perished in the forest and deserted the Law. Others, more fortunate, have safely crossed those dangers under the protection of Masters, and have seen the victims, and known where and why they fell. All pilgrims are liable to these

---

1. The sacred shrine at Makkah.

dangers. If one secures the help of a mighty Teacher, one can be saved and progress with the help of His secret hints and instructions, else one may fall into some heresy and lose the fruit of one's labor.

4. The pilgrim may pass, on the way, through certain spiritual conditions, and the soul may put off the physical garment, catch the reflection of the Divine Light, display superhuman powers as a Divine agent during the continuance of the experiences, taste the relish of "I am God, the Holy One," and become proud of having reached the goal. The pilgrim cannot understand this intellectually: but if the soul, during the continuance of these experiences, is not helped by a mighty Master, he may, it is feared, lose faith, and fall a victim to a false notion of unity.

5. The pilgrim on the way unfolds supersensuous powers, and sees supersensuous phenomena—devilish, passional, and divine. But he cannot understand them, as they are spoken in a supersensuous language (*i.e.*, revealed through an unfamiliar medium).... If, at this stage, he is not aided by a Teacher, helping him on behalf of God, and versed in the interpretation of supersensuous words and symbols, he cannot progress further.....

When God opens the eyes of a man, so that he distinguishes good from evil, and resolves to follow the one and avoid the other, but does not know how to do it, he must betake himself to a Divine Man and make a firm determination to change his condition. Then the Divine Man will take him up, help him to subdue the desire-nature, gently induce him to abstain from his defects and blemishes, and keep him away from bad companions. A disciple can, with the help of a Teacher, do in an hour what he would do unaided in a year.

It is said: a disciple may reach the goal with the help of a single Teacher, or of more than one Teacher. (In the latter case) each Teacher may be the means of the revelation of one stage only;

yet it is more consistent with decency and politeness for the disciple to refrain from looking upon such a stage as the limit of development attained by his Teacher,... inasmuch as the Perfect Ones are not at all concerned with the business of stages and conditions. But one cannot leave one Teacher for another without the permission of the former. Who does so deserts the Path.

It is the practice of the Masters—blessed be They!—to impose a threefold discipline on a student. If he observes it, he receives the Robe (the real one, not the conventional—else he is rejected. The threefold discipline consists of: 1. Service of the world for a year. 2. Service of God for a year. 3. Watching the heart for a year.—*Letter 5.*

ON THE QUALIFICATIONS OF A TEACHER

Broadly speaking there are five qualifications:

(1) Devotion to God. One cannot be thus devoted, unless one is free from servility to all save Him.

(2) Capacity to receive truths direct from God without any intermediary. One cannot unfold this capacity without completely getting rid of the lower human nature.

(3) Nearness to God. One cannot approach God unless one is equipped with the Divine character, and one's Spirit reflects the light of the Divine attributes.

(4) Acquisition of knowledge form God without any intermediary. For this the heart should be cleansed of all impressions—sensual and intellectual.

(5) Being an Elect of the Heart Doctrine, which relates to the knowledge of the Divine Essence, the Divine Qualities, and the Divine Works. One cannot attain to this stage without a second birth. "One born of the mother's womb sees this world; one born

of the Self (*i.e.*, quitting the lower human nature) sees the supersensuous world."

Nevertheless it is said that the qualifications of a Teacher are indescribable and innumerable. A Teacher is not the body, the head, or the beard, visible to man. He is in reality the inner being by the side of God, in the region of Truth, clothed in Divine mercy and glory... Here is a query: How can a beginner find out such a Teacher and Guide, know and follow Him? It is not meet for a beginner to weigh Divine Men with the balance of his little intellect and to look at Them with his limited vision. Nor is it meet to follow another on his mere assertion. Then how to know if such a one is a genuine Teacher or a mere pretender?

Answer: Each seeker is furnished with materials appropriate to his lot. He cannot transcend them, ... nor can anything hinder him from using them.

Query: Is there any sign whereby to distinguish a pretender from a true Teacher, the worthy from the unworthy?

Answer: There are many signs, but it is impossible to describe and fix them. For all-that, there is no sign or mood, the presence or absence of which *alone* would mark a Teacher or a pretender. In short, one blessed with the Divine Grace should set his feet on the Path, turn away from sensual pleasures and passional gratifications, and fix his attention on God. Then the glance of some Perfect Teacher will shine in the mirror of the heart ... When a true disciple catches such a glance, he instantly contracts a love for the Beauty of His Godly Strength, becomes restless and uneasy, and comes to the Path. This uneasiness forebodes fortune and success. Perfect discipleship consists in perfect love for the Beauty of the Teacher's Godly Strength. A disciple should follow the wishes of his Teacher, and not his own wishes... In each locality there is a Teacher who protects men living in that area. The King of the time is only one, but there is an ordinary teacher in each town. According to tradition there are always 365 Friends of God, who are the props of the world and the channels of the transmission of blessing and mercy from heaven to earth... O brother, know for certain that this work has been before thee and me (*i.e.*, in bygone ages), and that each man has already reached a certain stage. No one has begun this work for the first time. Everything is according to Divine dispensation. Do you suppose 100,024 prophets to have ushered any new work into the world? By no means. They stirred up what lay already in the bosom, and led man to what was ordained for him by God...—*Letter 6.*

ON DISCIPLESHIP

Desire is a craving in the heart for a certain object. The craving produces a stir in the heart; the stir arouses a tendency to seek for the object. The nobler the object, the purer the desire...

Desire is threefold:—

(1) Desire for the world. It consists in the absorption of a man in the seeking of worldly objects. Such a desire is a downright danger. When it clouds the heart of a neophyte, it keeps him back from all virtues, and lures him to failure. A life spent in the gratification of such a desire deprives one of eternal happiness after resurrection.

(2) Desire for heaven. The soul transcends the previous stage, longs for the heavenly state and permanent happiness, and practises lifelong asceticism, so that he may attain his object on the day of resurrection. The desire for heaven is nobler than the desire for the world...

(3) Desire for God. A man (at this stage) unfolds the inner sight, aspires to transcend the created universe, and considers it

disgraceful to seize anything contained in that area—so that he develops a longing for the Creator Himself and is respected in heaven as well as on earth. When a disciple ceases to hanker after the world and heaven, and regards everything save his Object as a hindrance to his (onward) march, he should heartily endeavour to seek God, come manfully to the Path, and resort to a compassionate Teacher, so that the latter may help him in treading the Path, and tell him of its dangers, thus securing him a safe journey without any break or failure.

The Teacher cannot turn an unruly candidate into an earnest disciple... If the spirit of the Path lies latent in a candidate, it will unfold by His company and service. The Divine Law works in this way.

ON DISCIPLESHIP (*CONTINUED*)

When a man calls himself a disciple, he ought to justify the title to the fullest extent and firmly tread the straight Path. He should constantly use the collyrium of turning back (Taubãh), put on the robe of detachment from connections and from self, drink the wine of Seeking out of the cup of Purity, draw the sword of magnanimity from the sheath of Religion, dismiss the cravings of the infidel Desire, practise absorption, and not care for the higher or the lower worlds. When he has become proficient in the truths of discipleship and the subtleties of Seeking, has gathered the fruits of purification and asceticism, begun to tread the Path and passed through several stages of the journey—then, if asked whether he is a disciple, he can say: "I may be one, God helping." Thus is discipleship justified, and pretension avoided.

This is the way of those endowed with insight and divine Wisdom. Not to look to personality at any stage, nor to depend upon its possessions. Many saints with a life-long devotion have slipped down from dizzy heights... A disciple who concentrates in himself the purity of all the angels and the piety of all men is self-conceited and sure to fall, if he knows himself to be better than a dog..... The beginner has a tongue, the proficient scholar is silent—*Letter 54.*

A disciple is a worshipper of his Teacher. If his rest and movements are in accordance with His commands, he is a disciple; if he follows his own desires, he is a follower of his desires, not of his Teacher. A disciple is he who loses himself in the Teacher. He shakes off his desires, as a serpent casts its sloûgh. If he has even the least remnant of desire left in him, and doubts and protests find room in his heart, he is a worshipper of himself, not of the Teacher... A disciple should be a worshipper of the Teacher, so that he may become a worshipper of God. One who obeys the Messenger verily obeys God—*Fawãed-i-Ruknî.*

God has concealed precious gifts under the difficulties He has imposed upon these men (*i.e.*, the disciples). A disciple should manfully discharge his duties without fail, in spite of the hardships and trials of the Path. God does not work in one way only, and it is difficult to know which way will lead the disciple to Him—joy or sorrow, gifts or privation. There is a divine secret underneath all sufferings and enjoyments in the world.—*The Series of 28 Letters, Letter 1.*

"A long journey is needed to ripen the raw." As a fruit requires both sunshine and shadow for its maturity, so a pilgrim requires the dual experience—joy and sorrow, union and separation, presence and absence,—for his perfection.—*Ibid, Letter 5.*

There is no bar to the reception of the Divine Light. If there is any, it is due to lack of capacity. How can an unpolished mirror reflect an image?... The pilgrim needs patience and endurance, not hurry and unrest. God knows each man as he is, and sheds the Light when he deserves it—*Ibid, Letter 4.*

Contentment is a *sine quã non*; one without it should abandon occultism and go to the market.

The performance of duties to the best of one's abilities cannot be dispensed with, as it is necessary for the safe passage of the pilgrim. While sane, he should follow Truth. Truth in words and conduct is ever beneficial, never harmful—*Ibid, Letter 15.*

THE FRIEND OF GOD—(THE WALEE)

The Walee (or the Friend of God) is one who constantly receives the favours of the Deity, which consist in his being guarded against all troubles, the hardest of which is the commission of sins. As a Prophet must be sinless, so must a Friend be protected. The distinction between the two is this: The one is beyond the commission of a sin; the other is liable to commit a sin on rare occasions, but does not persist therein... The Friend is endowed with all possible virtues... Again, it is said, the Friend is he who does not fail in his duties to God and the universe. He does not serve through hope and fear of agreeable and disagreeable consequences. He does not set any value on his individuality.

A Friend may be either known or unknown to the people. If unknown, he is not affected by the evils of fame.....

A Friend is he who does not long for the world or for Heaven, who forsakes himself for the Divine Friendship and turns his heart to the True One.... The Friends are the special objects of the Love of God. Owing to their devotion, they have been chosen as the Governors of His Kingdom, the channels of His Activities, receive special powers, and are liberated from the bondage of the desire-nature. They do not desire anything save Him, nor feel attachment to anything save Him. They have been before us, are in these days, and will be till the end of the world.....

They are today the appointed Agents of God to serve as channels for the propagation of the messages of the ancient Prophets, and to govern the world—so that the rain may pour from heaven by Their blessings, that plants may grow from the earth by Their purity, and that the faithful may prevail over the faithless by Their strength.

Superhuman powers are a kind of idols in this world. If a saint is content with their possession, he stops his onward progress. If he turns away from them he advances the cause of his union with God. Here is a subtle mystery, and it is this: True Friendship consists in the rejection of all save the Beloved. But attention to superhuman powers and reliance upon them means the rejection of the Beloved, and satisfaction with something other than Himself.—*Letter 8.*

THE BROTHERHOOD OF FRIENDS

[There is a passage on the hierarchy of Divine Friends in Fawãed-i-Ruknî, another work of the author, which is translated below as a supplement to the present subject.—*Trs.*]

There are 4,000 Walees who are not known to the world. They do not know one another, nor are they conscious of their exalted position. They ever remain veiled form the world, as well as from themselves.

There are 300 Akhyãr (the Charitable or the Benevolent) who solve the difficulties of the world and keep the gate of the Divine Sanctuary. There are forty Abdãl (the Substitutes); 17 Abrãr (the Liberated); 5 Nujabã (the Pure); 4 Autãd (the Pegs); 3 Nuqabã (the Watchers); 1 Qutub (the Pole), also called Gaus, the 'Redresser of Grievances'. All these know one another and are interdependent for the discharge of their respective duties. (Total, 370—*Trs.*)

According to another authority (Majma-us-Sãerîn) there are 356 Walees ever working in the world. When one of them retires, another takes his place, so that there is never any diminution in the number 356. They are made up of 300+40+7+5+3+1. The One is the Qutub of the world, the preservation of which is due to His holy existence. If He retired without another to take His place, the world would fall to pieces. When the Qutub retires, one of the Three takes His place; one of the Five fills up the gap in the Three, one of the Seven fills up the gap in the Five, one of the Forty fills up the gap in the Seven, one of the Three Hundred fills up the gap in the Forty, and a man is posted to the vacancy in the rank of the Three Hundred—so that 356 ever continue working in the world, and every spot is blessed by Their auspicious Feet. Their outer life is similar to that of ordinary people, so the latter cannot know Them. Inwardly, They are united with God. Love, Friendship, and the Mysteries have to do with the within, not with the without. They (the Walees) are too strong to be hindered by earth, water, fire, air, plains and hills. Being in the East, They can see and hear men in the West. They can instantly go from the East to the West, come from the West to the East, go to and come back from Arsh (the Divine Throne). Theirs are many superhuman powers of like nature.

POLYTHEISM, AND THE FRIENDSHIP OF GOD

Polytheism is twofold:—

(1) The outer, which consists in worshipping a god other than the One Highest God....

(2) The inner, which consists in thinking of a being, other than God, as a helper at the time of need.

Some say that to see anything save Him, is polytheism for an Occultist.

Some say that to refer to any separated self in any way, to be inclined to do anything with one's own will, and to resort to one's own schemes and plans in any emergency, are all forms of polytheism....

The chosen Friend is he who is of God alone, both without and within. He neither acts nor thinks against [the Divine Will]. He does not mix with the desire-nature, forgets his services in the presence of the Master, and cannot do without Him.... He is so filled with Him in all respects—both without and within—that it is impossible for anything else to enter into him.... He loses his desire, will, and all individual qualities, and exists merely through God's Desire and Will. He gets what he wills—not because he wills anything other than what is God's will, but because his will is one with God's. Nay God unfolds His Will in him.—*Letter 9.*

LIGHTS

When the mirror of the Heart is cleansed of impurities, it becomes capable of reflecting the supersensuous lights. They appear in the beginning as flashes, but gain in power and volume as the heart becomes purer—manifesting [gradually] as the lamp, the flame, the stars, the moon, and the sun. The forms of flashes arise from ablutions and prayers....; those of the lamp, the flame and the stars, from the *partial* purity of the heart; that of the full moon, from its *perfect* purity; that of the sun, from the Soul reflecting its glory in the perfectly purified heart. A time comes when [the inner light] is a thousand times more luminous than the [external] sun. If [the visions of] the sun and moon are simultaneous, the latter signifies the heart reflecting the light of the Soul, the former the Soul itself. The light of the Soul is *formless*, but is seen behind a *veil* distorting the *idea* into the form of the sun.

Sometimes the Light of the Divine Attributes may cast its reflection in the mirror of the heart according to the purity of the later.... This Light distinguishes itself by a feeling of bliss in the heart, which shows that it comes from God and not from others. It is hard to describe this bliss. It is said that the Light of the Constructive Attributes is illuminative, but not scorching; that of the Disintegrating Attributes scorching, but not illuminative. This is beyond the comprehension of intellect. Sometimes, when the purity of the heart is complete, the Seer sees the True One *within* him, if he looks *within*, the True One *without* him, if he looks to the universe. When the Divine Light is reflected in the light of the soul, the vision gives bliss. When the Divine Light shines *without* the media of the soul and the heart, the vision manifests formlessness and infinity, uniqueness and harmony, the basis and support of *all* existence. Here there is neither rising nor setting, neither right nor left, neither up nor down, neither space nor time, neither far nor near, neither night nor day, neither heaven nor earth. Here the pen breaks, the tongue falters, intellect sinks into nothingness, intelligence and knowledge miss the way in the wilderness of amazement—*Letter 12.*

THE UNVEILING OF THE SUPERSENSUOUS

The essence of the Unveiling lies in coming *out* of the veils. The seer perceives things not perceived by him before. The "veils" mean hindrances keeping one back from the perfect vision of the Divine Beauty, and consist of the various worlds—according to some, 18,000 in number, according to others, 80,600—all present in the constitution of man. Man has an eye correlated to each world, with which he observes that world during the unveiling. These worlds are included under a twofold division: Light and Darkness, Heaven and Earth, Invisible and Visible, Spiritual and Physical,—each pair expressing the same sense in different words.... When a sincere pilgrim, impelled by his aspiration, turns from the lower nature to follow the Law, and begins to tread the Path under the protection of a Teacher, he unfolds an eye for each of the veils uplifted by him, to observe the conditions of the world before him. First, he unfolds the eye of intellect and comprehends the intellectual mysteries to the extent of the uplifting of the veil. This is called the *Intellectual unveiling*, and should not be depended on. Most of the philosophers are at this stage and take it as the final goal. This stage transcended, the sincere pilgrim comes to unveil the heart, and perceives various lights. This is called the *Perceptual unveiling*. Next, he unveils the Secrets; this is the *Inspirational unveiling,* and the Mysteries of creation and existence are revealed to him. Next, he unveils the Soul; this is the *Spiritual unveiling*, and he can now view Heaven and Hell, and communicate with the Angels. When the soul is completely cleansed of earthly impurities, and is thoroughly pure, he unveils Infinity and is privileged to gaze at the circle of Eternity, to comprehend instantly both Past and Future, getting rid of the limitations of Space and Time,.... to see both fore and aft .... to read hearts, know events, and tread on water, fire, and air. Such miracles are not to be relied on.... Next comes the *Innermost unveiling*, enabling the pilgrim to enter the plane of the Divine Attributes.... The Innermost is the bridge between the Divine Attributes and the plane of the Soul, enabling the Soul to experience the Divine vision, and reflect the Divine character. This is called the *Unveiling of the Divine Attributes*. During this stage, the disciple unfolds esoteric knowledge, revelation from God, His vision, His bliss, real absorption, real existence, or Unity,—according as he unveils the Divine Attributes of intelligence, audition, sight, construction, disintegration, stability, or oneness. Similarly one may think of other qualities.—*Letter 13.*

[The last two extracts tacitly refer to the following Sûfi classification of the human constitution:-

1. The Body (Tan), the brain-consciousness, or intellect correlated to the physical plane (Nãsût).

2. The Heart (Dil), the desire and the lower mind, correlated to the astral and lower mental planes (Malakût).

3. The Soul (Rûh), the higher mind, the Ego, correlated to the higher mental plane (Jabarût).

4. The Spirit (Sirr, or the Mystery), correlated to the spiritual planes (Lãhût)—*Trs.*]

ON THE SAME

[The following supplementary notes from *The Series of 28 Letters* may prove both instructive and interesting.—*Trs.*]

You say you hear certain words, but not from the organ of speech, or through the organ of sound. Speech and Sound belong to this world: what you hear belongs to Malakût—*Loc. cit.* Letter 10.

A pilgrim may hear the 'sound' in his body, nay, in the minerals, plants, and animals. But if he hears from them the same Zikr (*i.e.*, the sacred formula) as practised by him, it is but an echo of his practice—an imaginary phenomenon, not a real one: whereas, if he hears from them the Zikr peculiar to them, the phenomenon is real.... The universe being endless, the phenomena are endless.—*Ibid,* Letter 15.

Powers and phenomena are trials for a pilgrim. Regard them as obstacles, and never care for them..... It is a rare boon to pass from the Name to the Named.... The Vision of the Prophet Khezar foretells your success on the Path.... The odours, sacred and unearthly, experienced by you, pertain to the Malakût: how can you find their likeness on earth?—*Ibid*, Letter 16.

ILLUMINATION

There is difference between Divine Illumination and Soul-Illumination. When the mirror of the heart is cleansed of all impurities, and has become thoroughly clear, it may serve to focus the rays of the Divine Sun and so reflect the Divinity and all His Attributes. But this boon is not enjoyed by every clean heart. Every runner does not catch the game (lit., the antelope), but only he who runs *can* catch it....

A clean heart reflects some of the qualities of the Soul. If thoroughly clean, it may at times reflect all the qualities. Sometimes the Essence of the Soul—the Divine Viceroy—may display its nature, and assert "I am the True One" by virtue of its viceroyalty. Sometimes the whole universe may be seen making obeisance at the viceregal throne, and the soul may mistake the Divine Viceroy for God.... Such mistakes are common, and cannot be avoided without the Divine Grace and the help of the Teacher. Now to come to the difference:

(1) Soul-illumination conquers the lower nature temporarily, *i.e.*, so long as the illumination continues;—Divine illumination conquers it permanently.

(2) Soul-illumination is not inconsistent with the foulness of the heart, does not solve all doubts, nor does it impart the bliss of Divine Knowledge;—Divine illumination is the reverse of this.

(3) —Soul-illumination may induce pride, self-conceit, and egoism.... Divine Illumination does away with all these, and increases the fervour of Seeking.

'Illumination' and 'obscuration' are two words generally used among the Sûfis. The former means the unfolding of God, the latter means the infolding of God. These expressions do not apply to His Essence, since It is changeless. As when one finds the solution of a problem, and says, "the problem is solved"—the problem is not solved, but one's mind unfolds so as to grasp the problem; knowledge being called the solution of the problem, ignorance its obscuration—

so, when one sees all from God, and not from self, when Self does away with the lower nature and sees the Unknowable,—this is designated Illumination.—*Letter* 14.

DREAMS

First, a pilgrim passing through the *earthly* qualities sees in his dreams heights and depths, streets and wells, gloomy and deserted sites, water and mountains. *Secondly*, passing through the *watery* qualities, he sees greens and pastures, trees and sown fields, rivers and springs. *Thirdly*, passing through the *airy* qualities, he sees himself walking or flying in the air, going up the heights. *Fourthly*, passing through the *fiery* qualities, he sees lamps and flames. *Fifthly*, passing through the *etheric*, he finds himself walking or flying over the heavens, going from one heaven to another, sees the circling of the sky, and the angels. *Sixthly*, passing through the *starry* region, he sees the stars, the sun and the moon. *Seventhly*, passing through the *animal* qualities, he sees the corresponding animals. If he finds himself prevailing over an animal, it indicates his conquest over the corresponding quality. If he finds himself overcome by an animal, it denotes the predominance of the corresponding quality, and he should guard himself against it.

The pilgrim has to pass through thousands of worlds, and in each world he perceives visions and experiences difficulties peculiar to it.

O brother, the soul is for the Goal. It should boldly cry out: "Let me either cease to live, or reach the Goal."—*Letter* 16.

ON MISCONCEPTIONS

Many men fall from doubt and suspicion. A class of people say, "God does not need our worship and services and has no concern with our virtues and vices: why should we restrain ourselves?" Such a doubt arises from sheer ignorance, and supposes that the Law enjoins duties for the sake of God. No. Duties are for the sake of man alone.... An ignorant man of this sort fitly compares with a patient who, being prescribed a certain treatment by his physician, does not follow it, and says that his abstinence does no harm to the physician. He speaks truly enough, but works his own destruction. The physician did not prescribe to please himself, but to cure him.

A second class of men transgress the Law and depend on the Divine Mercy. God is both merciful and a chastiser. We find that there are many distressed and poor men in this world in spite of His Mercy and His mountains of Treasure, that not a single grain of wheat grows without laborious cultivation, and that no man can be healthy without food, water and medicine. As He has ordained means for health and wealth without which they cannot be had, such is the case in the moral sphere also. Denial and ignorance are poisons to the soul, and idleness its disease. The antidotes for the poisons are knowledge and wisdom alone. The remedies for the disease are prayers and worship alone. He who takes poison while depending on the Divine Mercy, kills himself. The disease of the heart consists in desires. He who does not restrain his desires risks his life if he knows them as sinful. But if he does not regard them as harmful he has no life to risk, since he is already dead. For such disregard is denial, and denial poisons faith.

A third set would understand by self-discipline, as imposed by the Law, complete freedom from lust, anger and other evils. When they fail after practising self-discipline for a length of time, they regard the task as impossible. "Man, as he is constituted, cannot be pure, just as a black blanket cannot turn into a white one. Why should we undertake an impossible feat?" (So they think).—It is ignorance and vanity to suppose that the Law enjoins complete freedom from lust and other impulses inherent in human nature. The Prophet has said, "I am a man, and may be angry," and signs of anger were at times visible in him. God praises one who controls anger, not one who is devoid of anger. Again, the prophet had nine wives, and a man destitute of the sexual desire should be medically treated. The prophet has countenanced the begetting of progeny and the perpetuation of the race. But he has instructed that the two (lust and anger) should be subdued so as to be under the control of the Law, as a horse under the control of the rider, or a dog under the control of the hunter. The animals should be trained, else they will set upon and overthrow the man. Lust and anger are like the dog and the horse, and it is impossible to catch the heavenly Game without them. But they should be under control, else they will destroy *us*. In short, the object of self-discipline is to break and subdue these impulses, and this is possible.

A *fourth* set proudly declare that everything is according to the Divine Will. What is the use of exertion?—When the prophet spoke of the Divine Will, his companions said, "We shall depend upon it and retain from exertion." The prophet replied, "*Ye shall exert*, and [then] what has been ordained will be given." Thus, man should not refrain from exertion. If he has in the beginning been ordained to a noble destiny, he will attain to it [by exertion]. Good and evil destinies hinge upon virtue and vice, in the same way as health and death upon food and starvation.—*Letter 18.*

THE OUTER AND THE INNER AILMENTS

Man has been formed of two different substances, the earthly and the heavenly. As his earthly frame is liable to ailments, so is the heavenly; and there are doctors for the treatment and cure of both. The doctors of the bodily ailments are the physicians, and those of the moral ailments are the Prophets and [later on] the Saints who are their successors. As a sick man would certainly die if not treated by a skilled physician, so a soul suffering from the moral diseases would certainly die, if not helped by a prophet or a perfect Saint. As a physician examines the pulse to ascertain the disease of a patient, and recommends him to resort to one thing and abstain from another, with a view to restore physical equilibrium and health,—so also the Divine Messenger ascertains the moral ailments of the disciple, and prescribes different duties based on the Law according to his receptivity and capacity, recommending this, disallowing that, so as to reduce his inner perplexities and desires to a state of harmony required by the Law, and bring about moral health in the shortest possible time. As a sick man going against the instructions of his physician gets worse and worse and has to die, so a moral patient disobeying the Law gets more and more perverse and has to perish through ignorance.—*Letter 19.*

THE ORIGIN OF THEOSOPHY

The institution of Theosophy (Tassavvuf) is ancient. It has been practised by the prophets and the Saints. As evil impulses predominate in the world, the Theosophist (Sûfî) is looked down upon by men. The Theosophist is one who has lost the self, exists in the True One, is beyond the reach of the lower nature, and is at one with Truth. A Theosophical student (mutasavvif) is he who seeks to become a Theosophist through asceticism and purification, and disciplines himself in the ways of the Theosophist...

The prophet had a place in his mosque set apart to discourse privately with his elect companions, who trod the Path. There were senior disciples such as Abu Bakr, Omar, Osman, Alî and Salmãn;

and mediocre ones, such as Bilal and others. The Arab chiefs and his ordinary companions were not admitted there. The elect companions were about 70 in number. When the prophet wished to show his special regard to a particular companion (Sûfî), he favoured him with a piece of his garment (N.B. The word Sûfî may be derived either from Safã, purity, or from Sûf, dress.—*Trs.*)

The first Theosophist was Adam, and the last Muhammad; and Theosophy has continued amongst the followers of Muhammad.—*Letter* 22.

SEEKING THE PATH

The aspiration of the Seeker should be such that, if offered this world with its pleasures, the next with its heaven, and the Universe with its sufferings, he should leave the world and its pleasures for the profane, the next world and its heaven for the faithful, and choose the sufferings for himself. He turns from the lawful in order to avoid heaven, in the same way that common people turn from the unlawful to avoid hell. He seeks the master and His Vision in the same way that worldly men seek ease and wealth. The latter seek increase in all their works; he seeks the One alone in all. If given anything, he gives it away; if not given, he is content.

The marks of the Seeker are as follows. He is happy if he does not get the desired object, so that he may be liberated from all bonds; he opposes the desire-nature so much, that he would not gratify its craving, even if it cried therefor for seventy years; he is so harmonised with God that case and uneasiness, a boon and a curse, admission and rejection are the same to him; he is too resigned to beg for anything either from God or from the world; his asceticism keeps him as fully satisfied with his little all—a garment or a blanket—as others might be with the whole world.... He vigilantly melts his desire-nature in the furnace of asceticism and does not think of anything save the True One. He sees Him on the right and on the left, sitting and sitting and standing. Such a Seeker is called the Divine Seer. He attaches no importance to the sovereignty of earth or of heaven. His body becomes emaciated by devotional aspirations, while his heart is cheered with Divine Blessedness. Thoughts of wife and children, of this world and the next, do not occupy his heart. Though his body be on earth, his soul is with God. Though here, he has already been there, reached the Goal, and seen the Beloved with his inner eye.

This stage can be reached only under the protection of a Perfect Teacher, the Path safely trodden under His supervision only.... It is indispensable for a Disciple to put off his desires and protests, and place himself before the Teacher as a dead body before the washer of the dead, so that He may deal with him as He likes.

Virtue and vice have their uses and evils. Often a virtue throws one the farther from God, and a vice leads one the nearer to Him... The virtue that begins in peace and ends in pride throws one the farther from God; the vice that begins in fear and ends in repentance leads one the nearer to Him.—*Letter* 23.

THE PILLARS OF THE PATH

Their words enliven the heart; their deeds liberate men; their compassion is universal; they do not care for feeding and clothing themselves, but feed and clothe all; they do not look to the evil of others, but stand as their saviours, return good for evil, and bless them that curse. Why?—For they are protected: no gale save the zephyr of Love can blow over the world from the horizon of their heart. Their compassion shines as the sun over friend and foe alike. They are humble as the earth, trodden by the feet of all. They are not hostile to any man, nor do they grasp at anything of the world. All creatures are their children, they are not the children of any.

They are absolute Compassion for the whole universe, for east and west,—for they are liberated and see all from the One Root.... One void of these qualities cannot tread the Path.

In the case of a Theosophist, the heart goes first, then comes the tongue. In the case of a worldly-wise man, the tongue goes first, and then the heart.—*Letter* 24.

RELIGION, THE PATH AND TRUTH

Religion (Sharîat), the Path (Tarîqat) and Truth (Haqîqat).

Religion is a way laid down by a prophet for his followers, with the help of God. All prophets equally call the attention of men to Monotheism and Service. So there is but *one* Religion, *one* appeal, and *one* God. Their teachings cannot be contradictory, as they are based on Divine inspiration. The difference is merely verbal and formal, but there is no difference in the essentials. They are the [spiritual] physicians of humanity, and have prescribed religions for their respective followers according to their needs. Religion consists of a series of injunctions and prohibitions, and deals with monotheism, bodily purification, prayers, fasts, pilgrimages, the holy war, charity, and so on.

The *Path* is based on religion, and consists in seeking the essence of the forms [dealt with by religion], investigating them, purifying the heart, and cleansing the moral nature of impurities such as hypocrisy, avarice, polytheism, and so on. Religion deals with external conduct and bodily purification; the Path deals with the inner purification.

Religion is the soundness of external purification. *Truth* is the soundness of the inner condition. The one is liable to alterations, is the work of man and can be acquired; the other is immutable, the same from the time of Adam to the end of the world, and is the Divine Grace. The one is like matter, or the body. The other is like spirit, or the soul.—*Letters 25 and 26.*

[A higher stage is simply mentioned, in *Fawãed-i-Ruknî*, as Mãrfat (the Divine Knowledge), without any detailed explanation. Thus, Sharîat corresponds to the exoteric religion of any given nation; Tarîqat to the Lesser Mysteries of the ancient Western mystic, or the Probationary Path of the Eastern mystic; Haqîqat to the Greater Mysteries of the ancient Western mystic, or the Path Proper of the Eastern mystic; Mãrfat to the stage of the Perfect Man, or the Master—*Trs.*]

ACCESSORY TO PRAYERS

After the morning prayer, the twilight should be spent in muttering the Divine Names, sacred recitations, repentance and apology. One should not speak at this time, except to obey an express injunction or prohibition of the Scriptures, to bless or benefit the faithful, and to instruct a student in need of knowledge. The company of a Saint, a knower of God, or one's own Teacher, if available, is preferable to mutterings and recitations.

Before the sunset prayer, some time should be spent in attentively examining the desire-nature *i.e.*, reviewing the gains made and the losses incurred during the day.

One should go to sleep pure, and with holy recitations, and should not sleep unless overpowered. One should get up in the latter part of the night before twilight, and immediately take to the sacred duties.—*Letter 28.*

PURIFICATION

It is purity which makes man respectable. It is the storehouse of all boons and virtues.... Islãm is based on purity, and cannot tolerate the slightest stain. She does not show her face to the impure.

First:—the purity of the body, the garment, and food.

Second:—the purity of the senses, *i.e.*, abstinence from sins and transgressions.

Third:—the purity of the heart, *i.e.*, renunciation of all evil qualities, such as uncharitableness, envy and malice.

With the first purity, the disciple takes the first step on the Path; with the second, he takes the second step; with the third, the third. This is the essence of Taubãh—turning from impurity to purity. At first he was a temple of idols; now be becomes a mosque. At first he was a demon; now he becomes a man. At first he was dark as the night; now he becomes bright as day. It is now that the sun of Imãn (peace or faith) shines in his heart, and Islãm shows her face and leads him to the Divine Knowledge. Any work whatsoever, without this purity, is but a ceremony or tradition on the lines of the forefathers, but is *not* Islãm.

Know God as your constant guardian. Living under His ever-watchful Eye, one ought to be modest and feel ashamed to bring one's transgressions to His notice.

As prayers cannot be duly performed without the outer purity, so the Divine Knowledge is impossible without the inner purity. As fresh water—not water already used—is necessary for the one, so pure Monotheism—not mixed—is necessary for the other.[1]

The inner purification is hinted at in the prophet's prayer: "O God, purge out hypocrisy from my heart."—*Letters 29 and 30.*

---

1. See "Monotheism"—*Trs.*

THE MOTIVE

The value of a disciple's act lies in his motive. The motive is to the act as life is to the body and light to the eye. As the body without life or the eye without light is useless, so the acts of a disciple without a pure motive are mere forms. With the Seers, forms are denial and destruction, not faith and salvation. A valid motive arises from purity, as rays from the sun and sparks from the flame. When the motive is not biased by worldly attractions, it is called *ascetic* purity by the Sûfîs. When the motive is not biased by heavenly attractions, it is called *spiritual* purity. It is said that the motive of a man is according to his knowledge and wisdom. If desire and love of the world predominate in the heart of a man, all his acts will be worldly—even his prayers and fasts. If desire and love of heaven predominate in his heart, all his acts will be heavenly—even his eating and sleeping. Again there are others, of loftier aspiration, caring neither for earth nor for heaven, but for God only. All acts done by such men will be purely divine....

A disciple should always be careful to purify his motive and to get out of mere forms. For this, he should obey the instructions of a Teacher, His motive, though in the beginning mixed with hypocrisy and insincerity, will ultimately be purified by obeying His instructions.... The disciple should act as the earth, so that the Teacher may act as the sky—wet him with His rains, warm him with His sun, shade him under His clouds, perfume him with the fragrant breeze of His compassion—and thus help his growth.—*Letter 31.*

PRAYER

The daily routine of a disciple, in the absence of his Teacher, should be such as to secure purity of heart, whether by prayer, sacred study, mutterings, or meditation.

The secret of prayer is inexpressible. When the disciple, renouncing separateness, stands for prayer in a mood of self-surrender, his body ranks with Kãbã's shrine, his heart with Arsh (the Divine Throne); and his spirit sees the Vision Divine....

The devotee mostly prays with the fire of Love without observing external forms (*e.g.* kneeling and prostration), takes all devotees as one, and does not stigmatise any man with the brand of infidelity and damnation.

In the state of prayer, one merged in the Divine cannot be conscious of anything else; as Alî, while praying, was operated upon, and an arrow drawn out of his thigh, but he did not feel it.—*Letter 32.*

INVOKING THE DIVINE HELP

Opinions vary as to which is the better course, invocation of the Divine Help, or self-surrender to the Divine Will. In some cases the one is preferable, in others the other, according to the tendency and condition of each individual. If invocation induces *unfolding*, it is good. If it induces *infolding,*[1] it should be stopped. If it induces neither the one nor the other, its performance and omission are of equal value. If *knowledge* preponderates at the time of invocation, it is to be continued, for such an invocation is a worship in itself. If *Divine Wisdom* preponderates at the time, silence is preferable....

What is the use of invoking the Divine Help, if the Divine Will is irrevocable?—Answer: The revocation by invocation is also in accordance with the Divine Will, the invocation being simply an ordained means, as a shield is a means to repel an arrow, and watering is a means to grow seeds.

1. See p. 30.

If one resorts to an invocation, it is to be repeated three, five or seven times.—*Letter 36.*

THE DIVINE ALLEGIANCE

The Divine Allegiance gives freedom and the sovereignty of the whole world....

God never made anything so precious as the heart of His Servant, because it is their that He treasured up the wealth of His Wisdom: "I cannot be contained in heaven or earth, but I am contained in the heart of My faithful Servant."

What is Service?—To be resigned to the Divine Will without a murmur. A Servant is he who does not think of wages, and has been liberated from the bonds of desire. He who serves God for wages is the servant of the wages, not of God.

Khwãjã Hasãn Basri says: "Seek the Knowledge that is revealed by Service, and seek the Service that is revealed by Knowledge." Knowledge and Service are equally necessary, but Knowledge is superior, being the root and guide. Hence it is that the Prophet says: "Knowledge rules conduct, and conduct follows it." Again, He says that the sleep of the wise is better than the prayers of the ignorant, and that the ignorant do more evil than good by their acts.—*Letters 37-39.*

THE SACRED FORMULA

The disciple should ever practise the formula: "There is no God except Allãh"—vocally or inaudibly, whether he be alone or in company. Let him not for a moment step out of this fort. The fort is made of the negative "no God" and the affirmative "except Allãh" phrases; and it protects the pilgrim entering therein against the two highway robbers; the desire-nature and Satan. When the disciple unfolds the inner eye in the plane of Unity, he transcends affirmation and denial, as they are inconsistent with Unity. Affirmation and denial inhere in the nature of man, and a disciple does not attain to Unity unless he goes beyond human nature. Affirmation and denial are in themselves a form of polytheism, since a valid affirmation and a valid denial each need three elements—the affirmer, the affirmation and the affirmed; the denier, the denial and the denied. When a believer in *two* is a polytheist, how can a believer in *six* be a monotheist? When the non-God has no existence, what is to be denied? When thou thyself art not, how canst thou affirm?.... This is the zenith of Unity, and the stage of the Perfect Ones.... He who sees with the eye of Unity finds the non-God non-existent....

Whenever Muhammad, transcending the realm of His mission, looked with the inner eye into the realm of Unity, He eagerly and yearningly wished His personality blotted out, the dividing line erased, and the human limitation cast away. But the Compassion of the Beloved would ever intervene, and bring Him back to the realm of His mission for the delivery of the message.—*Letter 40.*

THE NAKED FAITH

Intellect is a bondage; Faith, the liberator. The disciple should be stripped naked of everything in the Universe in order to gaze at the beauty of Faith. But thou lovest thy personality, and canst not afford to put off the hat of self-esteem and exchange reputation for disgrace....

All attachments have dropped from the Masters. Their garment is pure of all material stain. Their hands are too short to seize anything tainted with impermanence. Light has shone in Their hearts enabling Them to see God. Absorbed in His Vision are They, so that They look not to Their individualities, exist not for Their individualities, have forgotten Their individualities in the ecstasy of His Existence, and have become completely His. They speak, yet do not speak; hear, yet do not hear; move, yet do not move; sit, yet do not sit. There is no [individual] being in Their being, no speech in Their speech, no hearing in Their hearing. Speakers, They are dumb; hearers, They are deaf. They care little for material conditions, and think of the True One [alone]. Worldly men are not aware of Their whereabouts. Physically with men, They are internally with God. They are a boon to the Universe—not to themselves, for They *are not* themselves.....

The knowledge that accentuates personality is verily a hindrance. The knowledge that leads to God is alone true Knowledge. The learned are confined in the prison of the senses, since they but gather their knowledge through sensuous objects. He that is bound by sense-limitations is barred from supersensuous Knowledge. Real Knowledge wells up from the Fountain of Life, and the student thereof need not resort to senses and groupings. The iron of human nature must be put into the melting-pot of discipline, hammered on the anvil of asceticism, and then handed over to the polishing agency of the Divine Love, so that the latter may cleanse it of all material impurities. It then becomes a mirror capable of reflecting the spiritual world, and may fitly be used by the King for the beholding of His own Image.—*Letter 41.*

THE INNER POLYTHEISM

The prophet says, "Polytheism in my followers is more imperceptible than the motion of an ant on a black stone on a dark night." Such a polytheism, though not affecting the [exoteric] faith, injures the essence and fruit of Faith. Pure gold and an alloy of gold are both gold, but the latter cannot be as precious as the former. True Faith consists in Monotheism, which is the antithesis of polytheism. Real Monotheism appears only when the root of polytheism[1] has been

1. Separateness.

destroyed. In order to secure true Faith or Monotheism, every impurity that stains it should be cast away. Such impurities constitute the inner polytheism. Looking to any save God for help or hindrance; hoping or fearing from any save Him; hypocrisy, anger and pride, even in their most subtile forms; pleasure and pain at being praised and blamed by others; regarding virtue and vice as means of union with and separation from God—all these come under the *inner* polytheism. In short, no one can be established in Faith unless his character comes up to the standard: "He is wholly from God, by God, and for God."

Again the prophet says: "There is no peace for the faithful except in the presence of God, and death is anything save His Presence."—*Letter 44.*

THE DIVINE KNOWLEDGE

Divine Knowledge is the essence of the faithful soul. One destitute of it does not really exist. The Knowledge of the Creator follows from the knowledge of created objects, and leads to the safety and permanence of the knower.

One way to the Divine Knowledge is to see the whole universe as subject to the Divine Will, to sever connection from all, and to realize the Unity of God and the Eternity of His Nature and Attributes.

Another is through one's own nature. "He that knows his own nature, verily knows his God." God first shewed His Powers in the universe to enable monotheists to gain Knowledge of Him by observing it. This way being too long for the Sages, He placed in Man the essences of the entire creation, thus making Human Nature the facsimile of the whole universe and the ladder to His Knowledge. Pilgrims tread the Path of Divine Knowledge *in* themselves, look for the pure and the foul *in* themselves, and find the indication and proof of that Knowledge *in* themselves.

God engages some men in observation, and they know Him by pondering over His creation. He leads others to His knowledge through asceticism. There is another class of men whose hearts He illumines at once. Again, some are debarred from the *essence* of the Divine Knowledge, others from the Path itself. "The Divine Beauty has thousands of aspects, each atom presenting some peculiar one."

Noori was asked: "What is the proof of God?" He replied: "The proof of God is God Himself." They asked him again: "Then what is the use of intellect?" He said: "Intellect is a failure, it cannot lead save to what is a failure like itself." Intellect can only look upon an entity either as *body, essence or accident*; or in Space and Time. It cannot go beyond those limitations. If it fixes any of those limitations on God, it sinks to infidelity. If, bewildered, it exclaims: "I do not find any existence save with these properties. So, God being without any of these properties, is perhaps naught,"—it is still dragged down to infidelity.... In short, Divine Knowledge depends upon Divine illumination alone.

Divine Knowledge is the knowledge of God as He is in His Essence, Attributes, and Works. The Sage should know God in the same way as God knows Himself, and as He has described Himself in the Qur'ãn. There are two theories as to the *perfection* of this Knowledge. Some Intellectualists hold that the Sage knows God in the same way as God knows Himself. If he does not know Him perfectly, he knows a part of Him. But God is partless. So sages are equal in Divine Knowledge. Intellectualists hold to the possibility of perfect Divine Knowledge. The other theory is held by the Sûfis and a few intellectualists as well, *viz.*, that no one knows God perfectly. They know Him to exist, and know it to the extent necessary for their salvation. They do not hold to the possibility of perfect Divine Knowledge.

With the Masters of the Path, Divine Knowledge is the actual and direct perception of God: with the Intellectualists, it is the sound intellectual knowledge of God.

It is incumbent on a pilgrim not to be satisfied and stand still until he reaches the Goal. The more he knows, the more he should seek.... The whole world is satisfied with a smell or a word (*i.e.*, very little), and no one has received even a drop from the holy cup. "I asked Him, 'Whose art thou with all this beauty?' He said, 'I am My own, for I am verily One. I am the Lover, the Beloved, and Love; I am the mirror, the image and the beholder'."—*Lett*

LOVE AND DEVOTION

This world and the next are intended to be used in seeking God. An objection raised against such a use of the next world is untenable: for prayer and fast, pilgrimage and the holy war, and all the exoteric obligations cease *as such* in the next world; but devotion—seeking after God—ever endures. If you go to heaven, each day of the heavenly life will open up new vistas of Divine Knowledge. An endless work is this, may it never end!

When God loves a man, He inflicts troubles on him and takes away his wealth, wife and children, so that he may be bound to naught, and estranged from all save Him. If he suffers patiently, he receives boons without toil. If he endures cheerfully, he is purified of all evils.

Again, God's love for a man makes him aware of the defects of his desire-nature, so that he becomes its instructor and censor.

The following are the signs of a man's love for God:—

1. Being given to prayer and seclusion.

2. According to others, preferring the Divine Word to human words, the Divine Presence to the sight of man, the Service of God

to the service of the world; and not grieving for any loss save separation from Him.

3. According to Junnaid: Not being tired in His Service.

4. According to a certain Sage: Avoiding sins.

It is dangerous to assert one's love for God.

The word "Mahabbat" (love) is derived from "Hibba" (a seed). The seed is the germ of life, as it is there that lies the real plant. The seed is put into the soil, lies concealed therein, and receives sun and rain, heat and cold, without any [apparent] change. When the time comes, it sprouts, flowers, and fructifies. So, when Love takes root in the heart, it bears presence and absence, joy and sorrow, union and separation, with equanimity....

Devotion is the perfection of Love. Worship make a servant, knowledge makes a knower, abstinence makes an ascetic, sincere seeking makes an earnest aspirant, sacrifice of all the world makes a Friend, self-sacrifice makes a Lover, losing the perishable and imperishable elements of self in the Beloved makes a Devotee.

It has been said: Devotion is born of the Light of the Presence of the Eternal Beloved. It is like a flash of lightning, illuminating the eye of the Devotee, speaking to his ear, enlivening his movements, and alienating him from all the world—so that his acts are not for self nor for others, but are works of impersonal Devotion to the Beloved.

Devotion is beyond words, intellect, and astral perception. "I am Devotion, beyond this world and the next; I conquer all without arrow or bow; I shine as the sun in every atom, yet my presence for its very brightness in unperceived; I speak in every tongue, I hear in every ear; yet, strange to say, I am tongueless and earless; as everything in the Universe is verily Myself, My like cannot be found therein".—*Letters 46 to 48.*

[The following extract from *Fawãed-i-Rukni* may appropriately find place here.—*Trs.*]

As prayers and fasts are the *outer* duties, so Love and Devotion are the *inner* duties. Their ingredients are pain and sorrow. Devotion leads the devotee to God. Hence Devotion is necessary to tread the Path. Know Devotion as Life, its absence as death. The privilege of Devotion is not granted to every man, nor does every man deserve it. He who deserves it is worthy of his God; he who does not deserve it is unworthy of Him. A Devotee alone can appreciate the value of Devotion. A vast multitude seek after heaven, while very few seek after Devotion; for heaven is the lot of the desire-nature, while Devotion is the lot of the Soul.

Get rid of the notion of selfhood, and give up thy self to Devotion. When thou hast done so, thou hast reached the Goal.

Dost thou know why so many obstacles have been set up on the Path?—In order that the devotee may gradually develop strength, and be able to see the Beloved without a veil.

The boat on the sea [of life] is Devotion; the Boatman is the Divine Grace.

SEEKING GOD

Nothing is more binding upon you than to seek God. If you go to market, seek Him. If you come home, seek Him, If you enter a tavern, see Him. If the Angel of Death come to you, take care not to neglect the Seeking. Tell him, "Do thou thy work, I do mine.".... If you be taken down to hell, you shall not neglect the Seeking. Say to the Angel of Hell, "Strike my useless personality with the whip of chastisement: I, on my part, tread the Path of Seeking"—so that the Work may go on. If you are taken up to Heaven, do not look to the *hooris* and palaces, but speed on the Way of Seeking. "Tho' they offer me both the worlds, I will not have them without Thy Presence."

The first stage on the Path of Seeking is *Humility*. The Great Ones say: 'Humility is the messenger from God to man.' Sown in the heart, it impels to God. Practised for some time, it turns into *Courage*. Masters unanimously hold that Love cannot put up save with the Courage of the Disciple. Practised for some time, Courage turns into *Seeking*. This Seeking is led by the Divine Will to the secrets of [the holy formula], "There is no God except Allah." The drum of Seeking proclaims at the gate of the Divine Sanctuary, "He who seeks God obtains Him." A cry resounds: "Let neither sky nor earth, heaven nor hell, hinder the path of My Seekers, for they seek Me, and I am their Goal." These are the steps on the ladder of human progress. Each pilgrim has his own stage, according to his aspiration.

The vigilant Seeker should kill out self-conceit and self-respect with asceticism and purification, transcend both the worlds, and be ready to lose his life. It is unlawful for him to aspire after anything in the universe. "One does not unite with the All, unless one parts with all."

It is said :

When Adam was lodged in Paradise, the Law commanded him not to approach the Tree, while the Path dictated to him to turn away from all. Adam said unto himself, "This Paradise is full of wonders, and I am its lord. But my heart longs to visit the abode of sorrow: lordship will not serve my purpose." A voice spoke to his spirit, "Adam, wilt thou remove to a foreign country?" "Yes," answered Adam, "for I have something to do." The voice said, "Do this work here." Adam : "The other is more important." The voice: "Heretofore, Paradise and the angels have been thy servants. Now thou shalt have to exchange the home of peace for the abode of condemnation, the crown for poverty, reputation for disgrace." Adam: "I accept all these, and will proclaim my freedom throughout the universe." So it cannot be said that Adam was deprived of Paradise, but rather that Paradise was deprived of Adam.—*Letter 50.*

THE WAY TO GOD

Khwãjã Bãyazîd was asked, "What is the way to God?" He replied: "When *thou* hast vanished on the Way, *then* hast thou come to God." Mark this: If one attached to the Way cannot see God, how can one attached to self see God?

When the Sun of Divine Knowledge rises, all modes of knowledge become ignorance; when Divine aspiration appears, all desires melt away.....

Whoever is bound to his exterior—his turban, his robe, the size and colour of his garment—is still attached to the personality and a worshipper thereof. Thou canst serve either personality or the Law: two contraries cannot unite. So long as you hanker after approbation and dignity so long as you become angry at an insult, you are with your old genius and self-conceit, and have not been accepted by the Law. You should sacrifice yourself in the Self. To no purpose do you change your dress and food. If you eat a single blade of grass in a lifetime, remain clad in a single garment for a thousand years, are shut up in a monastery away from the sight of men,—beware, lest you should be deluded. All these are but the subtleties of the desire-nature, its cunning and craft.

Many pious men are as motionless as a serpent or a scorpion frozen with cold. Their piety is not due to rectitude and purity, but to lack of opportunity. When summer comes in and the surroundings change, one may behold what they do.... No one can safely tread the Path without a Guide.... In the beginning, a disciple is not a fit recipient of the Divine Light. He is like a bat, unable to bear the light of the Sun. As it is dangerous folly to travel in utter darkness, he needs a lightless dazzling than the Sun, in order to illumine the Path for his safety. Such a light is that coming from the Masters, who, like the moon [reflecting the light of the sun], have become fit reflectors of the Spiritual Light.—*Letters 51.*

SPEECH AND CONDUCT

All learned men base conduct on speech. They have gathered their learning through the avenues of hearing and speaking. The Masters of Truth have received Their Knowledge through divine inspiration, which depends on following the Law. With Them, knowledge does not depend upon words or speech. It has no connection with the tongue. Knowledge is that which makes a man follow the Law. Secular learning deals with words. Knowledge deals with Truth, and is not to be found save in the region of the Real. The province of the tongue is letters, and they are limited. Knowledge comes from the Heart, and the Heart does not perish. God has not given Knowledge to all, whereas He has not withheld speech from any. Knowledge is that which controls desire and leads to God. That which contributes to the gratification of desire and leads to the courts of chiefs and oppressors is not Knowledge, but a snare. Knowledge makes one humble and frees from ostentation and disputes.... The end of all learning is the beginning of Discipleship.

The *first* robe worn by a Disciple consists in coming out of the self. The *second* robe consists in setting no value on what he heretofore took as divine, so that the flame of Discipleship burns all things in him. Then, he begins to see lights and utter charming words, leading to self-conceit and the admiration of others. This is snare of the desire-nature, and stops his progress. Here comes in the necessity of a Teacher to help him cross this stage and bring him from stagnation to motion. Thus *light is a thicker veil than darkness*. Hence is it that the Wise are dumb and blind, unaffected by the opinion of the people. Hence is it, again, that the difficulties of a Disciple cannot be solved by a learned man, as the latter is but versed in religion, while the difficulties of the former are connected with the Path. It is useless for a Disciple to follow the learned, as the dicta of the latter are concerned will *outer* conduct, while he has to deal with the *inner* life. The one is preparing for the destruction of self; the other seeks salvation for the self through knowledge. The business of the learned is to gather up what has been left by others, and store in his bosom the knowledge of the past. The business of the Disciple is to throw away and renounce what he has, and to unlearn what he has learned. So they are opposites and cannot be reconciled in any way.—*Letter 52.*

MAGNANIMITY

A disciple lacking in magnanimity makes no progress at all. One whose aspiration does not go beyond heaven, is not fit for this battle. The Wise hold that the desire to have everything in the world according to one's own wishes, befits a woman, not a *man*.... In short, a magnanimous disciple should first of all tread upon his own life, and try his sword on his own desire-nature, not on an infidel. For the infidel can only hurt the body, and plunder earthly possessions; whereas the desire-nature injures the very root of religion and destroys faith....

Be on the alert, and take no step without due caution, for Time is a penalty to the heedless.

It is said:—When a man wishes to enter the Path, the Chief of the Evil Ones, Satan, seizes his skirt and says: "I bear the Cross of Curse for this work, that no unclean fellow may enter the Path. If any dare come in without the Robe of Monotheism and sincere Earnestness, I lop off his feet."....

"Should thy inner eyes unfold, every atom would tell thee a hundred secrets. Then wouldst thou see each atom ever advancing. All are absorbed in the march—*thou* art blind—and the march goes on *in thee* as well. There is no limit to the progress of Love. Such *has been*, there is no help." From highest heaven to lowest abyss, all things are seeking and striving. It is the wicked man alone who has made peace with the enemy, and cut himself off from the Beloved.—*Letter 53.*

KNOWLEDGE

Knowledge is to purification and asceticism what ablution is to prayer. No practice is possible without knowledge, as no prayer is possible without ablution....

Knowledge is of two kinds: that received from teachers and books, and that unfolded in the soul. Again the latter kind is twofold:

(1) The Knowledge transmitted from the Divine Sanctuary into:

(*a*) The Soul of a Prophet. Such Knowledge is called Wahî.[1]

(*b*) The Soul of a Master. Such Knowledge is Ilbãm (inspiration).

(2) The Knowledge transmitted into:—

(*a*) The Soul of a Master from a Prophet.

(*b*) The Soul of a Disciple from a Master.

As a Master sees God in the Soul of a Prophet, so a Disciple sees God in the Soul of a Master.

---

1. A revelation received from God through an Angel (mostly Gabriel)—*Trs*.

"So long as the tablet of thy heart bears the impression of letters, thou dost not know any of the secret meanings. When the letters completely vanish from the tablet of thy heart, then comes the knowledge of the secret meanings."

Knowledge is the key to all virtues, as ignorance is the key to all vices. Knowledge ushers in liberation, ignorance brings in destruction. The celestial ranks and abnormal sacred powers spring from knowledge; chastisements in the various grades of hell result from ignorance. So the faithful should shun ignorance and the ignorant in the same way as vice and infidelity. "A wise man is my friend, and a fool is my foe." As ignorance and the ignorant are to be avoided, so is it obligatory to seek knowledge and the company of the wise—not worldly knowledge, but the moral; not the worldly wise but the morally wise. "If you acquire knowledge thoughtlessly, you will use it as a means of gaining worldly position. True Knowledge is that which leads to the Divine Sanctuary, not that which leads to wealth, rank and passional gratifications.' The company of a Sage for a day is more conducive to progress than purification and asceticism.—*Letter 55.*

[The following note may be added from "*The Series of 28 Letters.*"—*Trs.*]

Real knowledge comes from the Soul, and a true knower is he in whom lies the original and final Knowledge. The purer the Soul, the deeper and more subtile its comprehensions.—*Loc. Cit., Letter 6.*

THE STEPS OF A DISCIPLE

The first step is Religion (Sharîat). When the disciple has *fully* paid the demand of Religion, and aspires to go beyond, the Path (Tarîqat) appears before him. It is the way to the Heart. When he has fully observed the conditions of the Path, and aspires to soar higher, the veils of the Heart are rent, and Truth (Haqîqat) shines therein. It is the way to the Soul, and the Goal of the Seeker.

Broadly speaking, there are four stages: Nãsût, Malakût, Jabarût and Lãhût, each leading to the next. Nãsût is the animal nature, and functions through the five senses—*e.g.*, eating, contacting, seeing, hearing and the like. When the disciple controls the senses to the limit of bare necessity, and transcends the animal nature by purification and asceticism, he reaches Malakût—the region of the angels. The duties of this stage are prayers to God. When he is not proud of these, he transcends this stage and reaches Jabarût—the region of the Soul. No one knows the Soul but with the divine help; and Truth, which is its mansion, baffles description and allusion. The duties of this stage are love, earnestness, joy, seeking, extasy and insensibility. When the pilgrim transcends these by forgetting self altogether, he reaches Lãhût, the unconditioned state. Here words fail.

Religion is for the desire-nature; the Path, for the heart; Truth for the Soul. Religion leads the desire-nature from Nãsût to Malakût, and transmutes it into Heart. The Path leads the Heart from Malakût to Jabarût, and transmutes it into Soul. Truth leads the Soul from Jabarût to the Divine Sanctuary. The real work is to transmute the desire-nature into Heart, the Heart into Soul, and to unify the three into one. "The Lover, the Beloved and Love are essentially One." This is absolute monotheism....

"The motive of the faithful is superior to their acts." Acts by themselves are of no value: the importance lies in the heart.

It is said that the traveller on the divine Path has three states: (1) Action. (2) Knowledge. (3) Love. These three states are not experienced unless God wills it so. But one should work and wait. He will do verily what He has willed. He looks neither to the destruction nor to the salvation of any one.

One who wishes to arrive at the Truth *must* serve a Teacher. No one can transcend the bondage and darkness of desires unless he, with the help of the Divine Grace, comes under the protection of a perfect and experienced Teacher. As the Teacher *knowns*, He will teach the disciple according to his capacity, and will prescribe remedies suited to his ailments, so that "There is no God except Allah" be firmly established in his nature, and the ingress of the evil spirits be cut off from his heart. All the world seeks to tread the Divine Path. But each knows according to his *inner* purity, each seeks and aspires according to his knowledge, and each treads the Path according to his seeking and aspiration.—*Letters 56* and *57.*

[The following extracts from "*A Series of 28 Letters*" may throw further light on the subject. The Sûfî Mulk (or Nãsût,) Malakût, Jabarût and Lãhût severally correspond to, if they are not identical with, the physical, astro-mental, causal and spiritual planes of modern Theosophical literature.—*Trs.*]

It is not permitted to give out the knowledge gained through [supersensuous] vision. This much only can be recorded:—

The objects of the senses constitute this world (Mulk); those cognised by intellect constitute the plane of Malakût; the potentialities of all beings constitute the plane of Jabarût;.... In other words, this world is visible, the Malakût is supersensuous, the Jabarût is super-supersensuous.... The subtlety of this world cannot bear comparison with that of Malakût, the subtlety of Jabarût with that of the Holy Essence Divine. There is not an atom of this world but is permeated by Malakût; not an atom of Malakût but is permeated by Jabarût; not an atom of this world, Malakût and Jabarût but is permeated by God, and conscious of Him. Being the most subtile, He must permeate all—for the greater the subtlety, the greater the quality of permeation. Now you may understand the meaning of the verse: "God is with thee wherever thou art, and in thy very being, though thou mayest not see Him; nearer is He to thee then the nerve of thy neck."

1. *lit.*, walking or moving.

Hence is it said that this world, Malakût, Jabarût and God Himself are all with thee, and that the True Man is the focus and mirror of all the Mysteries of the Divine Essence. It is not permitted to go further lest exotericism may censure. "Utter not secrets before the mob if thou art a true devotee Hast thou not seen that Mansûr, intoxicated with devotion, uttered a secret and was put to death?"—*Loc. cit., Letter 2.*

ISLÃM

Islãm is other than the lower nature. So long as the lower impulses do not yield to purity, the heart has no affinity with Islãm. The investigators of Truth give to the bundle of the impulses the name of 'the desire-nature'. The outer body with its limbs and joints is not dangerous, but is simply a horse to carry the directions of the Law. God says: 'He sent us a horse from His mighty palace. Let us ride on it and come to the Path'. So long as it carries His directions we should not vex it. If it attempts to transgress the Law, let us punish it with the whip of asceticism, so that it may come back to the path. This is the discipline of the body. But if a man pricks his limb with a pin, saying that he thereby subdues the desire-nature, he is sinner. Many ignorant fellows labour under a delusion and foolishly take self-torture as an important discipline. By no means transgress the limit of the Law and common-sense. The body is a valuable horse, and fit to carry the divine charges. It is the desire-nature, and not the body, which deserves rooting out and chastisement.

The world is arrayed into two parties, the party of God and the party of Satan. Look well and see to which *you* belong....

A Knower has said, "No one comes to worship God, unless promised the bribe of heaven and threatened with the torture of hell." This indicates an indifference to Monotheism.

It is said:

On an Id day[1] Shiblî the Saint was seen mourning and clad in black. He was told: "This is the Id day. Why are you so clad?" He replied: "I see all men rejoicing and clad in new suits, but *not one* of them is aware of God. I mourn this day over their heedlessness." O brother, thou hast become inured to heedlessness, hast barred the gate of Divine Knowledge and art content with the gratification of desires. Rest assured, so long as thou dost not put off thy desires, thou canst not put on the robe of Faith; so long as thou dost not look upon the desire-nature as thy foe, Faith cannot come to thee as thy friend; so long as thou dost not cease thy connection with Satan, thou canst not see the beauty of "There is no God save Allãh"; so long as thou dost not turn from the world, thou canst not approach the Path of Purity.

Since the Lord is thy Origin, thou hast not come; since the Lord is thy Goal, thou wilt not go. "There is no God save Allãh." Nothing can be separated for the Infinite, and attached to non-God. Since the Origin is from Him, the End is verily in Him. Separation and union, coming and going, are thus unreal. This is a long story. Discreet silence is here absolutely necessary.—*Letter 58.*

THE NOBLE QUALITIES

Noble qualities were in the beginning of creation given to Adam, who left them as a legacy to other prophets. Muhammad, the head of the prophets, received them in His turn. Similarly, evil qualities were allotted to Satan who handed them down to his followers—the proud and the disobedient.... Since the Noble Qualities are the precious legacy of Adam to Muhammad, no garment or decoration is better for the faithful than that of the Noble Qualities. They are based upon harmony with the Divine Will and the Prophet's Life.

---

1. The Muhammadan festival day at the end of the Ramadãn fast.—*Trs.*

One should curb one's temper, lest it should embitter the life of others. One should ever be cheerful, and of controlled tongue. One should always salute others. One should be charitable, and abstain from slander, abusive words and untruthfulness. One should adapt one's words and deeds (*e.g.,* eating and sleeping) to the scriptural injunctions. One should ever be magnanimous and free from the taints of miserliness, hatred, greed and suspicion. One should do one's best to practise at all times the virtues possessed by the Prophet, and flee from vices.

The prophet has said: "Seek him who flees from thee; forgive him who injures thee; give to him who does not give to thee."

The prophet always concealed the defects of the faithful, and bore injuries and reproaches to propagate Religion. He was never angry for himself. He did not tolerate flattery, neglect, or silence in the service of Truth. He helped the friends when they were disabled. He worked for a servant in the family, when the latter was ill. He accepted the invitations and presents of others. He never found fault with any unprohibited food. He used any garment allowed by the Law—sometimes a blanket, sometimes a silk wrapper, sometimes a worn out cotton garment. He rode sometimes on a horse, sometimes on a camel, sometimes on an ass. Sometimes he walked on foot, without shoes, wrapper, turban or cap. He slept on a mat without bedding.... he had no miraculous power: His virtues were sufficient guarantee of His godliness. Many an unbeliever, just as he saw Him, would exclaim, "This is not the face of a hypocrite," and swear allegiance to Islãm without asking for miracle or argument....

The Noble Qualities are based on knowledge and insight. He who is fettered by self-conceit cannot be expected to purify his nature. Hence the pilgrim should use insight to acquire the virtues of the prophet. He should guard the virtues he has been endowed with, and acquire those he is lacking in by self-exertion (*i.e.*, asceticism, service, and the company of the saints). Most of the virtues can be acquired, and we have been ordered [by the Scriptures] to strive therefor to the limit of our powers. Man is a mirror who, when trained, perfected, and cleansed of impurities shows within him all the Divine Attributes of construction and disintegration. Then he realises his divinity and the purpose of his life. A Sage refers to this very fact in these lines: "It is thou who art the Divine Scripture: it is thou who art the mirror of the Royal Beauty. Beyond thee there is naught in the universe: seek thy object within thyself, for thou art that."—*Letter 59.*

CONTEMPLATION

The prophet has restricted the use of contemplation to the Works of God, not to His Nature and Attributes. Thinking on God may soon end in unbelief. In order that thought may work, its object must be limited, and the Divine Nature and Attributes are unlimited. Hence a student should contemplate on the objects of Creation, noticing their [relative] permanence and impermanence, and realising the position and changes of each in its phenomenal aspect. He will thus be led to the knowledge of the Creator. Hence the Seeker should [while not neglecting outward activities, holy recitations and other duties] contemplate from time to time on Creation—seeing the Wisdom of the Creator therein—, on his desires, on the heart and the body; he should enquire into his stages from the beginning of Creation to its end, and study his own character. His contemplation should be in conformity with Religion, based upon knowledge and experience, and irrespective of considerations of gain and loss, so that he may develop insight. Right contemplation achieves in a short time the results of long practice and worship. The prophet has said, "Contemplation for an hour is better than [formal] worship for sixty years."

As the range of the *outer* vision differs with different men, so is it the case with *insight*, or the *inner* vision. Some see as far as

Heaven, some as far as the Divine Throne. A few have the *perfect* insight which pierces through all Creation to the Creator.

The end of contemplation is the advancement of knowledge and the acquisition of wisdom. When the heart develops knowledge and wisdom, there is a change in its condition. With that change, there comes a change in conduct as well, and the man *turns*. With the *turning*, he begins to tread the Path. Treading attracts him to God. *Then* a current of Divine attraction may carry him to a stage inaccessible to men and genii by exertion and asceticism....

If thou longest and dost not succeed, be not dejected; for, as the Great Lord has said, "Asking is for men, acceptance for God."—*Letter 60.*

RENUNCIATION

The *first* duty incumbent upon a Seeker is the practice of Tajrîd and Tafrîd. The one is to quit present possessions; the other, to cease to care for the morrow. The *second* duty is seclusion, outer and inner. Outer seclusion consists in flying from the world and turning thy face to the wall, in order that thou mayest give up thy life on the Divine threshold; inner seclusion consists in cleansing the heart of all thoughts connected with the non-God, whether the non-God be earth or heaven.

The *third* duty is atonement in speech and thought, which consists in ceasing to speak and think of the non-God. The *fourth* duty is the practice of moderation in speech, food and sleep, since this triad supports the desire-nature. Too much speaking is a bar to holy recitations; too much sleep interferes with meditation; too much food brings on inertia and checks the performance of duties.

Purity of body as well as of mind is necessary at all times—purity of body *alone* is not sufficient—in order that the Divine

Attraction may uplift thee to a stage unattainable by *all* the efforts and ascetic practices of *all* genii and men put together. Very easy to speak of this, but very hard the practice—since this practice does not lie with the bodily organs or elements, but with the Heart and the Soul which are beyond our control. The gate to the Path is Knowledge and Wisdom. He who avoids this gate has to plod on his way through an endless forest infested by demons, and ends by losing his life and faith....

Eternal Life is the life in Spirit without a body. It is attained by Love, not by obedience. Servants wait for an order and seek remedies for their ailments; Lovers are impelled by Love and invite ailments without asking for a remedy. The Beloved ever cries, "Stay at a distance lest thou shouldst perish." The Lover answers, "I am prepared from the very beginning to give up my life. Death is better than a life without Thee." The life of the body has no value on the Path. Whoso cares for the one has no business with the other. Love says to thee: "Give up a life which must turn into dust, and I shall install thee on the throne of Glorious Atonement. Now the choice is thine."

Although there is no heart *without* love, yet the priceless treasure of Divine Love does not fall to the lot of greedy and mean fellows, who are content with prayers and fasts, and have but given up their earthly claims for higher honours.

Be cheerful and hopeful, for the Door of Compassion is open.

God has created doubt interfering with conviction, the lower nature veiling the face of Truth, duality warring with monotheism, the alloy claiming the place of the genuine coin, a thousand foes arrayed against each friend, a temple of idols facing every mosque, a suffering balancing each blessing, "He does all this; but man, awe-stricken, cannot breathe a sigh: for His Face is like a mirror, and a mirror is clouded by breathing."—*Letter 61.*

ON THE SAME

Tajrîd and Tafrîd are indispensable for a Disciple. The one is the renunciation of the world and of outer concerns; the other is the renunciation of self. No impurity in his heart, no burden on his back, no market in his bosom;—not reckoned with any class of people, not concerned with any particular object, his aspirations soaring above earth, heaven and the Divine Throne,—such a Disciple rests in his Beloved. The Beloved away, all the worlds cannot please; their absence leaves no void when He is there. As said by a noble soul, "No grief in the company of God; no joy in the company of the non-God." One away from God is at the very centre of sorrow and suffering, albeit he may hold the key of all the treasures of the earth. One attached to God, however poor, is king of heaven and earth. Khwãja Sirrî Saqtî was wont to pray: "O God! punish me, if such be Thy Will, any way save by veiling Thyself." This is the only real hell.... As observed by some one, "With Thee, the heart is a mosque; without Thee, 'tis but a shrine of idols. With Thee, the heart is a heaven; the heart without Thee is a hell."

In short, when the Disciple realises the Greatness of God, feels the pangs of His seeking, knows that "Who gainst Him gains all, who loses Him loses all," and finds that he can dispense with all save Him,—he then overcomes his old habits and unfolds the vision, "I am from God and for God." Life and death, acceptance and rejection, praise and blame, are thenceforth equal in his eyes. Heaven and earth find no place in his heart. He bows to none for food, clothes or money. His Goal being the Divine Sanctuary, he longs for naught save God.—*Letter 62.*

THE CLEARING OF THE PATH

The Path should be cleared of all impurities inherent in the lower self.... The Great Ones have declared: "He that takes a step in obedience to his desire-nature loves it better than God. He cannot be a believer: how can he be a Saint?"

Nothing but constant *turning* (Taubãh) can guard the Path against the onslaughts of the desire-nature. As the ordinary soul should turn from sensuality, cruelty and avarice, so should the developed soul turn from purity, worship and meditation. The Sages have said: "Thou must acquire all virtues, such as truth, purity and worship. When acquired, thou must scatter them in the air of supreme Indifference. Were all Prophets, Saints and Angels to sing the hymn of His Unity, their final chorus would end thus: "We turn to God from all we have said."[1]

Art thou endowed with the purity of all the Saints, plume thyself not over it; art thou distressed with a thousand shocks, seek not refuge in flight.

He that does not burn himself here in the fire of Taubãh certainly deserves the doom of hell-fire. So burn thou today in the fire of Taubãh whatever thou knowest of thyself, be it merit or defect. If to-day thou dost not cast aside the thorns from thy Path, they will hereafter turn into arrows and pierce thy heart.—*Letter 63.*

SELF-CONTROL

The Self-controlled is one who has freed himself from the bondage of self. The seven hells and the eight heavens are too narrow to hold him—only the vast expanse of God is wide enough to receive him.

If the joy of heaven and the torture of hell ceased to be, there would be no loss to the spiritual aspect of God. "What a Vastness! If the worlds were not, It would not be less by a hair's breadth. The kingdom of its Glory is truly without beginning or end."

1. Or "We retract with repentance what we have said."—*Trs.*

Freedom from self leads to freedom from all. So long as thou art bound to any of the lower qualities, thou art its slave.... The Path is a jealous master and will not put up with any partner. So long as thou art a friend to self, thou art a stranger to God. Be then estranged from self that thou mayest unite with Him. The dead wall of self cannot be pulled down save with the help of a perfect Teacher.

Self-control will not allow thee to look down upon any creature, *e.g.*, to tread upon even the lowliest ant in thy way. Wert thou able to raise the veil of ignorance from thine eyes, then wouldst thou see each and every being seeking and adoring God.

The prophet prayed, "Show me things as they are." His senior disciple ever prayed: "O God, show me truth and untruth, and help me to follow the one and avoid the other." So it is said : "When God seeks the welfare of a man, He shows his defects to him," that he may change from a temple of idols into a mosque.

Rest assured that thou hast nothing but good to expect, once self has been stripped off from thee. So long as thy self lies before thee, thou canst but swell in self-respect. A Satan in very truth is he that respects self, whether in the guise of angel or of man, whether on earth, in heaven or in hell. Self-respect consists in not transcending self. "Endless as the veils are, none is thicker than self-conceit. Know its destruction as thy foremost duty."—*Letter 64.*

TRUTH

Khwãja Zunnoon of Egypt says: "Truth is the Sword of God on earth. It may not be laid on anything without cutting it." Truth consists in looking to the Actor, and not to His instruments True Faith consists in ceasing to desire anything save Truth....

Once upon a time Zunnoon, while returning from Jerusalem, saw a figure loom in the distance, and desired to question it. On drawing near, it was found to be an old woman clad in wool, with a stick in her hand. Zunnoon said, "Whence comest thou?" The dame replied, "From God." Zunnoon again enquired, "Whither dost thou go?" The old woman rejoined, "To God." Zunnoon then offered her a gold coin. She refused the gift, saying, "What an illusion has overcome thee? I work for God and do not receive anything save what comes from Him. As I worship Him and Him alone, I cannot receive what is not Himself and comes from other than Himself." Having spoken thus, she vanished. Such is to be the ideal of the aspirant.

Working for God alone is the test of true devotion. Some think they work for Him, but they work for Themselves. They have conquered the desires of this world, but they seek for fruits in a higher world. A few work irrespective of all consideration of internal suffering or celestial joy, in pure love to carry out the Divine Will. "The earth is a place of suffering, heaven is a place of joy. We shall not receive the fruits of either, even to the measure of a barleycorn." It has been said. The virtuous often prove more selfish in their virtue than the sinners in their sin. The gratification of the latter is but transitory, the joy of the former is permanent. God does not gain by the self-denial of men, nor does He lose by their sensual gratifications....

It is an old adage, that the mere description of a savoury dish only intensifies the misery of hunger. Take an onward step if you can: lose your head and giver up your life.

As God is essentially One, a true believer must be a monotheist. Look for the proof, of this in the holy *Logion*, one half of which, "There is no God," separates [the believer from the non-God], while the other half, "Save Allãh," unites [him with God.] One unites with God in proportion to one's renunciation of the non-God. He who claims to have Faith should look at his own heart. If his heart flies from the non-God, his claim is genuine. If it longs for anything save God, and shrinks from the means of Divine Union, let him weep over his faith. Either he has already lost it, or is about to do so.

A certain Great One has said: "All men claim to love, but if the claim is carefully scrutinised, 'loving' turns out to mean 'being loved.'" True love consists in the complete renunciation of all desires. If one looks for the gratification of a desire, one plays the part of the beloved, not of the lover.—*Letter 65.*

THE DESCENT FROM ADAM

The pilgrim justifies his descent from Adam when he enters the Heart. Now he has finished the Turning, and begins his Pilgrimage. By the virtue, of his complete Turning, anything coming in contact with him undergoes a change. This is the power of Transmutation. This explains the phenomena of transmutation wrought by many Darveshes (*e.g.*, the change of wine into an innocuous beverage). Such a pilgrim may lawfully lay his hand on the imperial treasury, and use the wealth of kings. (Religious injunctions vary with circumstances. It is reported in the traditions that a young man came to the prophet and asked if he could lawfully take a certain oil in the fast month of Ramadãn. He said, "No." Next followed an old man who put the same question. He said, "Yes". The companions of the prophet were confused, and asked, "How is it, O Messenger of God, that you allowed in the one case what you prohibited in the other." He replied: "The one was a young man, and I was afraid of the fire of his youth; the other was an old man, and I did not apprehend any danger for him.") But those who take to the *outer* conduct without having reached the *inner* stage, court their own ruin. Such a stage must have the sanction of Divine Authority.

A time comes to the Master of the Heart, when all His limbs become [as sacred as] the Heart. No part of his body, *e.g.*, a nail or a hair, should be cast aside, as it partakes of the sanctity of the Heart. The broken hairs of the prophet were divided by His companions as a precious gift amongst themselves.... Hence arose the practice of sharing among disciples the pieces of the teacher's worn-out mantle. The practice is a mere sham if the teacher is not a Master.

He who has completed the Turning and reached the Heart, is a Master. Only such a one is entitled to the honour of a leader,—not one who is below this stage.

Question:—How to distinguish the real Master from a mere pretender?

Answer:—The *true* Seeker has an *inner* eye enabling him to recognise a real Master. He would not be attracted to a pretender. Dost thou not behold that if different kinds of animals flock together, and different kinds of food be placed before them, each will fall to on his own appropriate food and turn away from what is meant for others?....

The true Seeker also is known as *such*, as his inner eye opens to the vision of the Master, and he receives the nourishment suited to his aspiration. The Master begins to work on him. He is [as one] dead, and the Master give him a wash[1], purifying him of all undesirable elements. This purification completes the Turning. Then he begins his journey on the Divine Path—which is called the Pilgrimage.

This is not devotion as ordinarily understood (*i.e.*, prayer, fast, almsgiving, etc.). Allegiance to a Master is in itself Devotion;

1. This refers to the practice of washing the dead body before burial or cremation—*Trs.*

progress on the Path is its fruit. A brief prayer, a day's fast, or a simple charity, performed or given in obedience to a Master's direction, are more beneficial than long protracted prayers, or splendid gifts, performed or given in response to the call of the desire-nature.

As a qualification for the Path, seek to get rid of old habits. But it is not possible to get rid of old habits and purify the dross without the service of a Master, since He alone can, by His Knowledge, gradually drive out the host of the evil elements, and help one towards the realisation of "There is no God save Allãh."

Continue thy seeking till *the* Seeking unveils Itself, and destroys thy self in Thee. Henceforth the Disciple has nothing to do: the Seeking will Itself lead him on.

So long as thou seekest any but the Beloved, no Seeker art thou. How then canst thou be wholly His? By wholly turning to Him. He can afford to have thousands of friends, for He can reach all alike. The Sun is with all—east and west, Hindu and Turk—for His range is unlimited. But *thou* art limited in capacity, and canst not feel the warmth of His rays unless thou wholly expose thyself to Him. All the worlds are benefited by Him; yet He does not lose in the least.

Here one should guard against a possible misunderstanding. To love a thing as a *means* does not interfere with the love for the *end* or the *final* object. Our foes even ought to be loved as connected with the Lord. This is not a division of love, but its perfection. Love is a peculiar stage: friendship with foes is possible only here. Abul Abbas—peace be on him—said to a party marching to war against the unbelievers, "Would I might lick the dust of the feet of the unbelievers whom ye would kill for His sake." The care of a scholar for pen and paper cannot be said to divert his attention from learning. The *real* object of love ought to be only one (*i.e.*, God), but loving others as subservient to the final object (*i.e.*, Divine Love) is by no means harmful. If a man loves God, he must love the Prophets and the Masters—nay, if he ponders well, he must love *all* as connected with Him. All the universe is His work and is certainly Himself. "Duality does not approach Thy Sanctuary: the whole world is Thyself and Thy Energy. The Universe is the shadow of Thy Presence; all is the result of Thy mighty Workmanship."

But if it be the Divine Will to put an end to a certain work of His, using thee as instrument, thou as a devotee must destroy it, and none should accuse thee of lack of respect for His work. This is a very high stage. If Muhammad and His blessed companions killed the unbelievers, they did so in obedience to the Divine Will. The lover has not to seek his own pleasure.—*Letter 66.*

CONFIDENCE

The Sûfî trusts in God. Khwãjã Yahiã observes: "He who does not trust God cannot receive Divine Illumination." *Explanation:* God deals with a man according to his expectations. One who suspects Him cannot receive any light. Again, it is a friend who is trusted, and it is a foe who is suspected. Suspicion invites hostility; confidence, love.

There is a distinction, however, between mere groundless hope and reasonable expectation. One who endeavours to obey the Divine Commands may reasonably expect the Divine Grace; but it is a vain hope for one guilty of commissions and omissions to expect exemption from hell and enjoyment of heaven.... So it is wise to check the accounts of the desire-nature, and prepare for death; and it is foolish to follow the desire-nature and hope for the remission of sins.—*Letter 67.*

PURSUIT AND RENUNCIATION

Sûfîs differ as to whether they should follow or renounce worldly pursuits. Complete renunciation is only permitted at a very high stage, *i.e.*, that of absolute unity and perfect trust in God.

Working for a livelihood began with Adam. He cultivated lands and taught cultivation to his children. The Prophet Shoaib was a merchant and possessed cattle. Moses served as His shepherd. If work interfered with the principle of trust in God, the prophets would not have worked for a livelihood. Muhammad warned his friends against the abuse of the principle of trust, and ever kept in store a year's provision for his children. Work is a duty for him who has to support another; but he should work so as not to be cut off from God.

Each should look to his circumstances and inner attitude, in order to decide whether he should resort to work or cease from work. If ceasing separates him from God, work should be resorted to; if ceasing leads him to God, work should be left aside.

Work is as lawful as prayer and fast. The more you pray, the more you fast, the better; but to look for your salvation therefrom is dualism. You should adore for the glorification of God and the strengthening of your love, but you should rely on His Grace for your salvation. Similarly, work is better than renunciation; but it is not the work, but rather the Divine Grace, which is to be looked up to as Providence.

A Dervesh should avoid begging as far as possible, as it is dangerous in many respects. He, however, may beg (a) to gratify his hunger.... (b) to pull down his personality.... (c) knowing the world as the Divine steward. It is more in keeping with the ceremonious glorification of the Lord to ask of His steward than of Himself.—*Letter 69.*

THE COMPANY OF THE SAINTS

Holy company is an important discipline for the pupil. It is very effective in conquering nature and habit. Hence is it laid down by the holy Saints as binding upon a disciple. The rationale of it is this. The desire-nature consists of certain ingrained tendencies, and is affected by the tendencies of one's associates. The Prophet says: "Men follow the religion of their friends, so they should always be careful of their company."....

It is said that a man, while going round Kãbã, prayed: "Lord, make my brothers virtuous." Others asked him, "Why dost thou pray for thy brothers at this sacred spot, and not for thyself?" He replied: "I have brothers who, when I return to them, will elevate me by their virtues if they are virtuous, and degrade me by their vices if they are vicious. As my righteousness rests on theirs, I pray for them, that they may help me in reaching the Goal."

Malik (Peace on Him!) says: "Do not associate with a brother or a friend, unless you would thereby advance the cause of Religion. To associate with any other object is absolutely forbidden." *Explanation*: If you associate with a superior, he will benefit you by his presence; if you associate with an inferior, you should benefit him by teaching him religion and morality, and yourself too by learning something useful he may know.

Company is to be sought for the sake of the Lord, not for selfish gratification.

Nothing is more dangerous for a beginner than loneliness. A story runs thus. There was a disciple of Master Junnaid who fancied he had made great progress and could not be harmed by isolation. So he took to seclusion. Nightly, a procession appeared before him with a horse for him to ride, and he was requested to ride up to heaven,—a delightful place with sweet dishes, running brooks and fair company—where he enjoyed himself till morn, and slept. On awakening, he would find himself at the door of his hermitage. He turned proud and boastful. On hearing the report, the Master came to him, asked him and was told what had happened, and advised him to repeat three times when he went to the pleasure-haunt: "There is nothing to be relied upon save God, and there is no power except His." He refused to act up to the advice for a few nights more. At last he wished to test the efficiency of the Master's lesson and repeated the sentence as advised. The whole procession fell into confusion and scattered, and he found himself in a cemetery with the bones of the dead around him. Then he came to realise his guilt, repented, and returned to the company of his fellow-disciples.

The rule of society is to behave with each according to his position in life. *With reference to elders*, to serve them; not to speak before them save when necessary, and then only with their permission, and after they have finished if they are speaking; not to sit on an elevated seat to their presence. *With reference to equals,* to live in harmony, and to share one's wealth with them not as a loan, but as a free gift). *With reference to the young*, to treat them with love and kindness.

General: Elders to be treated as one's own parents, equals as one's own brothers, the younger ones as one's own children. None to be asked for anything, but each to be helped. Life to be rendered agreeable to all. Not to oppose others except at the call of religious duty. To associate with those strong in religion, integrity and moderation. Not to mix with those opposed in religion and temperament. To avoid the company of a youth. (The desire in the young for the company of their elders aids the development of their intelligence and knowledge. The desire in elders for the company of youths leads to sin and folly)....

Sûfîs, when conversing with one another, never say, "This is mine," "That is thine"; "I wish it were so," "I wish it were not so". It is the verdict of the Masters of Knowledge that God does not approve of the use of words denoting I-ness.

If thou wouldst know the Unknown, taste the nectar of Grace and transcend the seven heavens, then close the five senses, and pass from the perishable to the Imperishable. They asked Master Shiblî, "Who is a Knower, and how is he to be distinguished?" He said, "He is deaf, dumb and blind." They replied, "These are the marks of an unbeliever." He rejoined: "The unbeliever is deaf to the voice of truth, dumb for the utterance of truth, and blind to the vision of truth; whereas the Knower is deaf, dumb and blind to all save Truth."—*Letter 70.*

SERVICE

Service is an essential duty for the disciple. Its gains are superior to those of worship. It kills the desire-nature; it breeds humility and good manners; it destroys pride, impurity and inertia, quickens the soul and illumines the inner and the outer man.

They asked a Great One, "How many ways are there to God?" He said : "There are as many ways as there are atoms in the universe. But the best and the shortest is Service. I have reached the Goal by treading this Path, and recommend it to my disciples."....

Rules of Service: To put aside one's own desires, to render oneself agreeable to other,.... and to regard one's powers and possessions as intended for the use of others....

As the wealthy are to serve with their wealth and the learned with their knowledge—so the disciple is to use *all* his activities for the service of others....

All Great Ones began with Service, which gradually lifted them to the rank of Masters.—*Letter 71.*

[The following notes gleaned form other works of the Author are added as bearing on the subject.—*Trs.*]

The outer conduct of an occultist should be in accordance with the mental capacity of the people surrounding him. He should speak what concerns them only, and not of his own relations with God. Master Yahiã observes: "When with others, I say 'My Lord'; when alone, I say 'My Beloved'; when united, I say 'I'." Obey the Law, whatever your stage or position. Such is the approved mode of conduct, as recommended by the Master of Wisdom.—*The Series of Letters,—Letter 21.*

A certain Great One was told that the chief of a certain town spend the whole night in prayers. He replied that the poor fellow had missed the way and undertaken the work of others. On being questioned again, he added that man's path of duty lay in feeding the hungry, clothing the naked, comforting the distressed, and fulfilling the wants of the needy; and that keeping up all night in prayer was the duty of a recluse. Each man ought to work according to his position in life.—*Fawãed-i-Ruknî.*

THE TRANSMUTATION OF EVIL QUALITIES

The purification of character by the transmutation of evil qualities into virtues is to be ever striven for as an essential duty. If neglected, it must breed dangers and difficulties.

Man has all the qualities found in the animals. His resurrection will be determined by his predominant quality, not by his outer body on earth—*i.e.*, he will turn into the form of the corresponding animal. For instance, the predominance of anger, lust, pride or flattery in earthly life, produces severally the forms of the dog, the hog, the lion and the fox, on the day of resurrection. Similarly of other qualities....

Many men will be seen in beastial form on the day of resurrection, and many beasts in human form. The dog of the Cave-recluses[1] will rise in the form of man, owing to his human qualities. Mount Ahud will have a rock drawn out of it, and will stand in the rank of the Pure Ones in human form.... Those endowed with the inner eye know that all beings, even the mineral, pray. "Every particle of dust in the air is full of the Light of Divine Love. All atoms in the universe are centres—active or potential—of Divine Love."

Such a difficult task lies in front, and none take to it save the Wise. So thou shouldst not be heedless, but slowly and steadily discipline thyself so as to overcome a part of thy animal nature—it is indeed a mighty achievement to overcome it in its entirety.

He who wishes to know the nature of his resurrection should see what is the predominating quality in his life: his resurrection will be determined by this quality. It is not difficult to know thus much.

Similarly, if a man wishes to know whether God is pleased or displeased with him, he should look at his life. A life wholly devoted to righteousness must please God: righteousness is the indication of His pleasure. A life wholly given to vice must displease God: vice is the indication of His displeasure. A life partly righteous and partly vicious is to be valued according to the predominating element in it.

If the earthly life is not turned to account, there shall be no progress on the other side. If a man who has not transmuted [on earth] the evil qualities in his nature, is taken to heaven at his death, and all celestial boons are bestowed upon him, those qualities will not change. He will have only the houries, the

1. The reference is to the seven sages who, with a dog, retired to a cave to avoid the persecution of a tyrant, awoke after a sleep of 300 years, and slept again to awake on the day of resurrection.—*Trs.*

palaces, the roast cocks and the stream of running water, but will be too weak to realise the real object—the Goal of the *inner* man, and the ideal of all the disciples and of the Master. How insignificant are all other gains where That is lost! How immaterial is any loss, where That is gained!

Frequent ablutions and baths remove sloth and drowsiness.

The Divine Vision on resurrection day depends on the Divine Grace, not on merit. No eye deserves His Vision, no ear His Voice, no intellect His Knowledge, no feel His Path.... Self-reproach is necessary for a seeker.—*Letter 72.*

AVARICE

To work for show, and desire the rank of a saint, is not the mark of piety. Thy deeds are all tainted with desire. Purity consists in the spirit of Service, not in avarice. The one is not compatible with the other. But we want bribes to serve the Lord.

O brother, cast off avarice. God does not owe anything to any one, and His gifts on earth or after death are gratuitious. Do all your works for His Service, not in the hope of gaining heaven or shunning hell....

He who aspires to work in His Service should be careful of the purity of his motives, which is a function of the heart. An act without pure motive cannot soar from the region of sham to the sphere of Service.... A prayer worth the name is one performed with the fervour of the heart, and not with the lips only. The motto of monotheism, "There is no God save Allah," if repeated as a talk at moments of sale and purchase, can not be regarded as a declaration of Divine Unity.... God says: "My shrine is not a place of sale and purchase. Thou goest to market with the object of gaining something thou hast not. But if thou comest to My

Shrine, come with the distinct understanding that thou losest all and returnest a pauper." Khwãjã Ahmad had a vision of God, Who told him: "Ahmad, all men ask Me for something, save Bãyazîd[1] who asks for Myself alone."—*Letter 73.*

THE EVIL OF THE WORLD

The world and all things therein are to be avoided, save as needed for the Lord's sake. The world may be classed under three groups:—

(1) The first group is purely worldly, and cannot serve His Cause. It consists of:

(*a*) Vices. Their commission in the mind or with the body does not serve His Cause.

(*b*) Too much of lawful enjoyments. This is the root of all failures and sins.

(2) The second group is purely divine, but may be turned to selfish use by an impure motive, *e.g.*, meditation, prayer and asceticism, if practised with the object of gaining the respect of the people.

(3) The third group is apparently worldly but really divine, *e.g.*, eating for the sake of the Divine Service; marriage with the object of begetting a child who shall repeat "There is no God save Allãh"; making a small fortune with the object of peacefully serving God.

In short, the world is that which gratifies the cravings of desire in the present, and is of no use after death; that which may help on the other side of death is not worldly.... He who appropriates the world to the limit of *bare* necessity (food, garment and a dwelling-

1. A great Muhammadan saint.

house) breaks his bonds; whereas he who seeks luxurious living exposes himself to endless troubles....

The Great Ones have remarked that the lowest stage of purity shows itself as an inner craving for well-being after death and a diminution of worldly desires, ending in a gradual estrangement from this world, and the realisation of other worlds....

The work is harder than you imagine. All worldly pleasures are sorrows and sufferings.—*Letter 74.*

RENUNCIATION OF THE WORLD

Service of the Lord is impossible without renunciation of the world. When thy body works for the world and thy heart longs for it, how canst thou serve Him? The heart is one; it cannot attend to two things at the same time. The world and the Lord are wide apart as east and west. The more you approach the one, the farther you recede from the other.....

Renunciation is twofold:—

(1) Human renunciation, *i.e.*, the renunciation which can be achieved by a man. It consists of three stages:

(*a*) Ceasing to seek for the worldly objects one has not.

(*b*) Casting off the worldly objects one has.

(*c*) Ceasing to entertain worldly desires in the mind.

(2) Superhuman renunciation, which consists in complete indifference to the world. It can be accomplished, with the help of the Divine Grace, by one who has achieved success in all the three stages of Human renunciation. The second is the true renunciation with many Sages.

The expulsion of worldly desires from the mind is a most difficult task. You will find many cases of *apparent* renunciation, with an *inner* longing for the world. But when you cease to seek for what you have not, and cast off what you have, the Divine Grace will enable you to drive out worldly desires from your mind. Relinquishment of the world will not give *real* renunciation, so long as the heart still craves for the world. The prophets were master-ascetics. One of Them was Solomon, who possessed the sovereignty of all the worlds, and was certainly an ascetic.

Conclusion : The separation of the heart from worldly cravings, in spite of the possession of worldly objects, is superior to the separation of the body from worldly objects, in spite of the worldly cravings that remain in the heart.

Renunciation is the basis of all virtues and progress, and, as such, is the first condition of discipleship. Ahmad Hambal (Peace on Him!) say that renunciation is threefold:—

(*a*) Abstinence from what is forbidden by the Scriptures. This is the lower renunciation.

(*b*) Abstinence from over-indulgence in lawful pleasures. This is the higher renunciation.

(*c*) Renunciation of that which separates man from God. This is the highest renunciation.—*Letter 75.*

THE FINAL DOOM

There are two classes of travellers, the noble and the wicked. Each class has its peculiar speed, path, and doom.

Noble souls are divided into ordinary noble ones, and the more advanced. The former attain heaven and the heavenly ranks by following the ascetic practices prescribed by Religion. The more advanced approach Purity by following the path of Devotion.

The wicked, too, are divided into ordinary wicked ones, and the more degraded. The former include some of the believers, leading a sinful life, disobeying the divine injunctions, and addicted to sensual pleasures. They tread the path of transgression and go to hell. The latter are the unbelievers, solely attending to sensual pleasures and earthly gains, and wholly disbelieving in Religion and the disembodied life. They risk the permanent for the sake of the transient, and finally lose this world as well as the next. The former suffer in hell temporarily, but finally escape it by virtue of their faith, albeit imperfect. The latter eternally suffer in hell owing to total absence of faith.

There are different gradations in hell, as there are grades of unbelief or hypocrisy. There are thinkers and blind followers amongst unbelievers as well as amongst believers. As the faith of a thoughtful believer is superior to that of an ordinary believer, so the sufferings of a thoughtful unbeliever are intenser than those of an ordinary unbeliever. Ordinary unbelief is inherited from ancestors and surroundings, and is punished in the first infernal region. Intellectual unbelief does not rest upon tradition, but upon researches carried on for long years, self-denial and discipline of the lower nature, all intended for and ending in scepticism and atheism.—*Letter 68.*

THE SOUL (RÛH)

People differ in their opinions on the Soul—some call it a body, some an essence, some an accident; some regard it as eternal, others as created. Orthodox Islãm declares its existence, but is silent on its nature and quality. God says: "If questioned on the Soul, say, 'It is from the Will of God.'" Abu Bakr Qahatî, however, holds that the Soul is beyond the category of created objects. [The author does not subscribe to this view, and enters on a controversy to show its heresy.—*Trs.*] —*Letter 79.*

[The following notes from *The Series of 28 Letters*, may be added as bearing on the subject—*Trs.*]

In search of peace, and fervently longing for spiritual fragrance, a pilgrim came to the Soul and said: "Thou art a reflection of the Glorious Sun, unfading; all the attributes of the Absolute One lie verily in Thee. Transcending Reason and understanding, Thou eludest description and predication. There is no creature above Thee, there is no Beloved beyond Thee." These lines from Master Farîd Attãr, and the hints underlying them, ought to be carefully pondered over—so that one may realise that there is no existence outside the Self, and that whatever one seeks is to be sought within the Self. If an authority be needed, one may read from the Qur'ãn: "He is within thee, though *thou* mayest not see." Again, this couplet is worth perusal: "Adam first ran towards all the atoms of the universe, but he did not find God so long as he found not the Way within himself."—*Loc. cit., Letter 24.*

The connection of the Soul with the body compares well with that of God with His universe: for the Soul is neither within the body nor without it, neither united with it nor separated from it. Soul and body belong to two different planes of existence; yet for all that there is not an atom in the body but is pervaded by the Soul.... The Soul retains its innate purity, linked though it be to the body for myriads of years.—*Ibid., Letter 3.*

THE HEART

There is a treasure buried in the heart of the knower. It is Love. A single jewel out of it is worth a thousand heavens. The guardian of heaven is an angel named Rizwãn, whereas the guardian of the treasure of Love is God Himself.

Know that thy merit is measured by what thou seekest.... If thou worshippest to obtain heaven or avoid hell, thou worshippest thy own desires. If thou seekest or fearest an object, thou art the worshipper of that object. Thy real value depends on what is in thy heart. If thy heart is attached to God, thou art a divine man....

Junnaid, when ill, prayed for his recovery. A Voice answered him, "Dost *thou* come in between Myself and Thee?"

Thou walkest every morning to office and comest back at dusk. Where is the difference between thee and the fire-worshipper and the Jew? Thy prayers are for increase of wealth, and thy pilgrimages for popular approbation. All thy acts are similarly tainted with name and form. The real end of life is yet veiled from thee.—*Letter 80.*

NAFS, THE DESIRE-NATURE

Some say the desire-nature is a substance, placed in the body, similar to the Soul. Others say it is a quality of the body, similar to life. But all take it as the source of evil qualities and acts. These evils are grouped into : (a) sins, (b) qualities, *e.g.*, pride, envy, anger. The former pertain more to the *outer* man, the latter more to the *inner* man. The former are purified by ascetic practices, the latter by Taubãh (or Turning)....

It is said that the desire-nature and the Soul are both mysterious entities in the body, corresponding to demons and angels, hell and heaven in the macrocosm;—the one being the centre of evil, the other the centre of Good. There is no help against the desire-nature save in ascetic practices.

Man is the epitome of the Whole Universe, and is composed of the Soul, the desire-nature and the body. He bears the characteristics of all the worlds. The earth, water, fire and air of this world appear in his body as the four humours: blood, phlegm, melancholy and bile. Other worlds are not less vividly marked in him. The Soul leads him to heaven, being its image; the desire-nature leads him to hell, being its image.

Bû Alî saw his desire-nature in the form of a hog. He wished to kill it, but it said to him, "Do not trouble thyself: I belong to the Army of God, *thou* canst not annihilate me."

Muhammad Nûrî speaks of his desire-nature coming out of his throat in the form of a miniature fox. "I knew it was the desire-nature, so I put it under my feet and began to trample upon it. It grew the larger and the stronger. I said, 'Pain and torture destroy all things, but they simply aid your growth!' It said, 'This is due to the fact of my constitution being the other way: what is pain for others is pleasure for me.'"

Abul Abbãs saw it in the form of a yellowish dog. When he attempted to turn it out, it came underneath the skirts of his garment, and disappeared.

Abul Qãsim saw it in the form of a serpent.

Another Dervesh saw it in the form of a mouse, and asked who it was. It said, "I am the death of the heedless and the salvation of the Divine Friends. If I were not, they would turn proud of their purity and noble deeds."

These stories go to show that the desire-nature is a corporeal being—not a quality—albeit it is endowed with qualities. It should be subdued by ascetic practices, but it cannot be completely destroyed in its essential nature. There need not be any fear from its existence, when it has been subdued by the disciple.... This dreary forest cannot be crossed save with the help of the Divine Grace and under the protection of a Master of Compassion.—*Letter 81.*

DESIRE

'Desire' is a term covering all the qualities of Nafs. It prevents union, tortures the disciple, and stands against the seeker. It is to be opposed and not to be gratified. "He who follows it is ruined; he who opposes it attains his object."

Desire are twofold: (*a*) those connected with the senses and sex; (*b*) ambition of power and fame. The victims of the former resort to brothels without seriously affecting the well-being of others. The victims of the latter resort to holy places, and become the pests of the world. They isolate themselves from society and mislead others. He who seeks the allegiance of his desires is far away from God, be he above the sky; he who renounces his desires is in close touch with God, be he in a heathen temple.

Master Ibrãhîm says: "I went to see a Jewish monk in Turkey, who had confined himself in a temple for seventy years. He opened a window and said he had not shut himself up there to secure the position of an ascetic, but to break the dog within him and restrain it from harming the world at large. I praised God for showing the right path to his misguided devotee. He went on, 'Ibrãhîm, how long will you seek men?—Seek the self, and watch it when found. The desire-nature constantly puts on many a semblance of divinity, and invites man to his ruin."....

It is said of Master Abû Alî that he wished to cut off his genital organ, as the root of lust, when his eyes fell on it while bathing. A Voice whispered to his soul, "By My honour, no organ is better or worse than another in My eyes. If you lop it off, I can put in each hair of your body the whole lust of your genital organ." It is no use destroying the organ: it is a vehicle for carrying the divine command. But a man can transmute its quality, God helping.—*Letter 82.*

THE DISCIPLINE OF THE DESIRE-NATURE

The desire-nature is the worst foe. It is very difficult to be armed against it, since, firstly, it is an *internal* foe, and it is almost impossible to guard the house against a thief co-tenant; and, secondly, it is a *lovely* foe, and a man is blind to the defects of his beloved, whose shortcomings take on the appearance of merits. Such being the case, the desire-nature may ere long hurl a man unawares to the lowest depth of degradation. If you ponder well, you will find it at the root of all the troubles what beset man in the past or may beset him in the future. This being the foe, one should intelligently strive to overcome it. It is improper to overcome it *all at once*, as it is a vehicle and instrument of the Soul; nor is it proper to let it go wholly unbridled, in view of the probable dangers. So the disciple needs a middle course, and it is this: You should strengthen it to the extent of enabling it to perform its duties; you should weaken it to the measure of preventing the chance of its leading you astray. Anything besides this rule is objectionable. It is reported in sacred tradition that on seeing Abdullãh Masûd, who had by ascetic practices weakened his body, his feet having become incapable of motion, his eyes having sunk in their sockets, Muhammad said, "O Abdullãh, be warned! Thy desire-nature has claims on thee." So the conclusion is that the desire-nature should be disciplined by knowledge, so that it may neither overcome (nor disobey) thee, nor be itself destroyed.

The middle course consists in restraining the desire-nature by temperance. There are three ways of thus subduing it: (*a*) withholding gratification;.... (*b*) imposing religious observances; (*c*) invoking the Divine help for mastery over it. If you follow this threefold method, the desire-nature will be amenable to discipline.—*Letter 83.*

DISCIPLINE OF THE DESIRE-NATURE (*CONTINUED*)

The discipline of the desire-nature is recommended by all creeds and nations, and is known by Sages as a means of developing the supersensuous faculties.... But thy business lies with the discipline only, it is God's to grant supersensuous faculties. Thy labours cannot bear fruit without His Grace. Avoid as much as possible the thought of personality and its activities, and never follow the promptings of the desire-nature. It is thy existence that veils Thee. Had there been the veil of a single activity, it could be uplifted by another opposite activity. But *the whole* of thyself being a veil, thou canst not be fit for the Divine Vision, unless and until *thou* vanish completely. It should not be forgotten in this connection that the discipline of the desire-nature means the transmutation of its qualities, not the destruction of its essential nature—for *that* is impossible. But its existence need not be regarded as dangerous after it has been subdued by the inner Ruler.

Fasting is recommended by all nations and creeds. It helps the receptivity of the heart, the purity of the intellect, and the health of the body. Regulation of food is an important work. It is food that imparts strength and weakness, purity and foulness to all the organs of the body. It must be pure in quality and moderate in quantity. —*Letter 84.*

ALIENATION FROM THE DESIRE-NATURE

Alienation from the personality is the first step to acquaintance with God. The one is a necessary condition for the other. All aspirants find fault with, and impose tasks on, the desire-nature, o that this wall of separation be pulled down, and a way be found to the Divine Sanctuary.

So long as thou lookest down upon a single soul as inferior to thee, thou art self-conceited, and blind to the Divine Presence.

"If thou hast knowledge, put that knowledge into practice; solve thy difficulties by knowledge and practice (combined)."....

The knowledge of all the Sages culminates in the realisation that they do not know.

There has been a single Master of Woe in each cycle, protecting others under his charge. On the path of asceticism, a considerable amount of prolonged exercises is a necessary preliminary to initial success, which, too, is doubtful. On the other hand, he who is trained on the Path of Woe has for his first stage the Purity of Devotion....

Be of good, cheer, in spite of thy lack of devotion and the heavy weight of thy sins. "Never despair of the Divine Grace"—it affords protection to all sinners. Poor as thou art at present, do not be dejected: "The Lord has created a beautiful form for thee," and "made Man after His image."—*Letter 85*.

SELF-TOLERATION

He who is on good terms with the self is dead, though apparently living; he whose life is in God is really living, though apparently dead. Death is not of the body alone: the *inner* man may die in the same way as the *outer*. Men are perishing in the sea of desires. Their Saviours are the prophets who help them to cross the sea of desires and merge in the Divine Unity.... The ungodly live in the form only and are dead in the *spirit*, since true life consists in human nature responding to the Divine Life. On the other hand, "Those who have sacrificed themselves on the Path of God are not to be considered as dead, but as living with their Lord."....

"The Divine treasury is too full of prayers already. Put in a grain of humble devotion if you can."—*Letter 86*.

HIDDEN DIFFERENCES OF STAGES

Men differ, in the gradations of their progress, as heaven from hell, though they are so similar in their outer forms. All men—whether in the past, the present or the future—are the centres of mysteries. Each body treasures a Divine Secret; each Heart feels impelled to the Path; each Soul radiates a glow unfathomable by human and angelic intelligences.... The best and holiest men had an obscure life.

Once upon a time Zunnoon sent a disciple of his, to enquire about Bãyazîd. When the disciple reached the latter's house at Bustãm, he found him seated on the floor of his cottage. But he did not know that he was Bãyazîd. Bãyazîd asked the disciple what he wanted. He said he wanted to see Bãyazîd. Bãyazîd replied: "Which Bãyazîd do you want, and whence? Now I am Bãyazîd, yet I have been in search of Bãyazîd for several years, and to no effect." The disciple took him for a madcap, and, returning, reported the matter to Zunnoon. Zunnoon with tears in his eyes exclaimed: "Our brother Bãyazîd has gone forth into God with the true Devotees"....

There was one Helãl, a slave to Mogîra. On his death the prophet with his companions went to the house of Mogîra. The latter was not even aware of the death of Helãl, for none took care of him, alive or dead, as he was the lowliest in the household. Mogîra came to receive the party and kissed the blessed feet of the prophet. The prophet asked Mogîra what had happened in the household. He said that all was well. The prophet went on: "Mogîra, the worthiest of your household has departed, and you do not know of it." Mogîra astonished, remarked "I never supposed Helãl to have been so advanced".... The prophet was then (at His request) taken to the place where the dead body was. He found it in a stable at the feet of the beasts, clasped the head and said with tears in His eyes: "Helãl, thy body lies on this earth, but thy Soul is with the Lord." All the saints and chiefs then wished in earnest devotion to have been the dust of Helãl's feet. The prophet continued: "There are seven men in each cycle who support the world by their blessings and lead the faithful to victory by their magnanimity. Helãl was the Head of these."—*Letter 87.*

HEEDLESSNESS

Heedlessness is blamed by all creeds and sects. It is heedlessness that lies at the root of all failures.

It has been said. When a man heedlessly approaches the Path, the Devil warns him, saying: "I was the Teacher of the celestial Hosts, but I lost that post. Now I guard the Gate of the Path. You may enter with the pass of Devotion only—else will you have to share my fate, being unfit for the Path"....

Everlasting purity is the character of the angel; lifelong transgression is the character of the devil turning with sorrow from sin to purity is the character of man. Lifelong purity is impossible for man. He is born imperfect, void of reason, with desires (the agents of the Devil) in full sway. Reason (the curb of desires and the light of the angelic essence) develops later—*i.e.*, after the capture of the heart by desires. Hence the necessity of Turning and self-discipline, *pari passu* with the development of reason, for the recovery of the heart from desires and the Devil.—*Letter 88.*

SORROW

No reading is so useful as that of the diary of sorrows.... The Goal is unattainable save through the destruction of the desire-nature. Either be ready to kill it out and tread the Path, or withdraw yourself from the rank of the seekers—so that others may pass on (unimpeded by your presence).

A Story.—David, when about to pray, saw an ant, and wished to remove it from the place. The ant appealed to David against his cruelty. David said: "God, how am I to deal with Thy creatures?" God replied. "Behave with self-restraint, lest thou shouldst harm any; do not look to the outer body of a creature, but to the Spirit underlying. An ant, if permitted, may rend asunder the dark Veil, radiate the Light of Divine Unity from its bosom, and put to shame many a monotheist."

Another Story.—Once upon a time, Moses prayed so warmly that the stimulating effect was felt by him till the succeeding day. He wondered whether any one could be so blessed as he was the night before. The angel Gabriel presently came with this message from God: "There is One, in this forest, who can cure the ills of My devotees." Moses hastened to the spot, and found a frog croaking in a pool. The frog said: "Moses, I have long been waiting to uproot pride from your heart. The Divine influence you felt last night passed through me. I received it first and then passed it on to you. Be warned against the repetition of the boast!"—*Letter 89.*

CONDUCT

An act not permitted by the Qur'ãn is fruitless; a desire not sanctioned by the prophet is vain. To wish for any help on the Path save that from the Path is forbidden. The Qur'ãn permits nothing save sincere conduct, and sincerity springs from the heart that has tasted pain....

The Masters of the Path are spiritual beings. Their word is life; the purity of Their sorrow vitalises the world; Their character is spotless....

So long as thou dost not unlearn all thy previous notions, habits and defects, thou canst not unfold the Eye of Wisdom in the Heart, and feel the relish of the Science of Truth.... He who is destitute of Divine Wisdom today (*i.e.*, on earth) will not have the Divine Wisdom tomorrow (*i.e.*, after death.)

Acts not based on Knowledge are futile; ascetic practices not countenanced by religion are misleading and devilish. It is Knowledge that unfastens the gate of good luck. It is Knowledge that can comprehend the greatness of Islãm, the mysteries thereof, the glorious character of the prophets, the sublimity of Their mission, the different stages of the advanced souls, the secret of the human constitution, the evil in the wicked, the respect due to Faith and the faithful, the injunctions and prohibitions of religions. Tread zealously the Path of Knowledge till you get rid of ignorance. Knowledge is the shortest way to God; and ignorance is the densest veil between thee and Him. As Knowledge is productive of Good, so is ignorance productive of evil. It is ignorance which brings in faithlessness, neglect of religious duties, affinity to the devil, alienation from the prophets and the Pure Souls, and other innumerable evils.

Seek no connection with the self, lest thou shouldst be affected with pride.... "Thou canst not reach Me, so long as 'thyness' inheres in thee: thou shalt reach Me only when thou quittest thy self." O brother, subdue thy desires with asceticism tempered by knowledge; cut off the head of the desire-nature with the sword of self-discipline, as advised by the Scriptures.... and (then) put on the robe of Islãm. If thou art really in earnest, tread upon thy life—so dear to thee—and do not fear death; what follows is Life, through and through. "If thou dependest upon (bodily) life, thou wilt lag behind. Thou art Life in the world of Life alone. Grasp well the subtle fact—thou *art* That which thou seekest." The foremost duty of the seeker lies in seeing the Beloved as the only Life, and in eliminating the evil of his own separated existence.—*Letter 90.*

SECLUSION

A man not wanted by the world for its intellectual or theological education, may isolate himself from others, and avoid company save on necessary occasions, such as those of the Friday and the Id prayers, a pilgrimage to Makkah, and other useful meetings. The man who wishes to avoid company altogether, had better live far away from human habitation (in a mountain or on a desert island). Else [let him not isolate himself altogether] unless he knows for certain that his gains from attendance at the Friday prayer or other social gatherings are really outweighed by the losses he incurs from coming into contact with human Society....

But there may be a different sort of man, a Master of Knowledge, needed by others for their religious enlightenment, the exposition of truths, the setting aside of heretical arguments, and for stirring them to live out the teachings of religion. It is hardly lawful for such a man to absolutely avoid human society. It is narrated of a Sage named Abû Bakar that, as he wandered about the hills with the object of leading a life of prayer and worship in seclusion, he heard a voice saying, "Abû Bakar, why dost thou desert the creatures of the Lord when thou hast attained the position of a Divine Light?" So he returned to the society of men.

Such a man, though living corporeally in the world and doing his duties to it, has to work for his own salvation as well. Omar (peace on him!) said of himself, "should I sleep at night I would ruin myself, should I sleep during the day, I would ruin my subjects." It is exceedingly hard to be corporeally in the world and to be at the same time mentally away from it.

Imãm Gazãlî opines that a learned man may be excused for isolating himself and burying his knowledge in days of trouble and degeneration, when a man may send for a religious teacher, but declines to learn anything of him—when no man appreciates the importance of religious duties....

An extremely weak man should not resort to seclusion....

The real object of seclusion is mental isolation, not bodily separation.—*Letter 95.*

DEATH

There are three classes of men: (1) The man of desires, (2) The beginner who is just turning back. (3) The advanced Knower of God.

The *first* does not recollect death; or if he ever does so, he does it in a spirit of sorrow for the loss of worldly objects, and begins to murmur at it. Recollection of death throws him the further from God.

The *second* is given to the practice of recollecting death, so that he may live fear-stricken, and accomplish his Turning the more successfully....

The *third* never forgets death, as it is the guarantee of his union with the Beloved.

But the highest stage of development is shewn in the soul that completely surrenders itself to the Lord, and foregoes all choice of life or death....

The frequent recollection of death is recommended, as it is calculated to disturb physical enjoyment, and thereby lead to salvation....

Death is welcome to the faithful, as it sets him free from the prison of earth-life and its tortures....

As remarked by an esteemed friend, earth-life is a state of slumber, the after-death life is a state of waking, and death is an intermediate state.....

Death (to an ordinary mortal) is more painful than a cut with the sword or the axe, or the extraction of flesh from his body....

A calm look, and the repetition of the Holy Formula, these are becoming on the part of the dying man.—*Letter 97.*

HELL

Every man is liable to suffer in hell, and it is difficult to be certain of exemption therefrom. According to the prophet, there are 70,000 apartments in hell, each apartment containing 70,000 doors, each door having 70,000 serpents and 70,000 scorpions; and the unbelievers and the evil-minded cannot help passing through each of them....

Such is the description of hell, and of its subdivisions which correspond to the number of earthly desires. The factor seven in the subdivisions corresponds to the seven organs used in the commission of sins.

If you wish to know your destiny, you should look at your character, since your natural inclinations presage your destiny. If they tend to good, you are not intended for hell; if they tend to evil, you are destined therefor. As the Qur'ãn says, "The virtuous are to be blessed in heaven, the vicious are to suffer in hell."

Here is a secret. When death takes away the earthly veil (the body), the desire-nature is yet more or less tainted with earthly impurities. In some cases the mirror of the soul may be too darkened to admit of any cleansing. Such a soul is eternally barred from the Divine Presence. In other cases, (*i.e.*, unrighteous believers), the rust is capable of being cleansed, and so the desire-nature is exposed to hell-fire to the extent of the purification needed. The time varies from a brief moment to 7,000 years. No man quits this earth without some impurity, however slight, in him.—*Letter 99.*

HEAVEN

Heaven contains apartments made of various gems, the outside of which is visible from the inside, and the inside from the outside. They abound with pleasures and comforts not tasted or conceived by men (on earth).... Heaven is a vast palace made of a single pearl. It contains seven apartments of red ruby. Each apartment contains seven rooms of green emerald. Each room is provided with a gorgeous seat, 70 trays and 70 maid-servants. Each seat has 70 beddings of different colours, and a Houri as the bed-maker. Each tray is furnished with 70 dishes.

Heaven is intended for those who salute and feed others, fast and pray....

When the dwellers of heaven wish to communicate with their brothers, their seats move the one towards the other. Thus they meet and talk of their past relationship on earth. There is procreation in heaven if so desired: conception, birth, and maturity all taking place instantaneously.

The dwellers of heaven are beautiful as Joseph, and well-behaved as Muhammad.

The duration of the lowest heavenly life is 500 years.

Such is the heaven of the ordinary soul.

Now as to the destiny of the prophets, the purest Devotees, and the Saints. Theirs is the vision of the Divine Face, in the supreme relish of which the grosser enjoyments of heaven are forgotten. Orthodox Islãm does not regard the Divine Vision as the fruit of human works, but as the result of Divine Grace. It holds a similar doctrine as to the Faith in the Lord of human beings upon earth.—*Letter 100.*

[The following brief Note is added from the *Series of 28 Letters.—Trs.*]

Imãm Qasherî, explaining the Secrets of the Qur'ãn, says:

"What the faithful will manifestly enjoy after death in heaven, is inwardly experienced by the Saints on earth."—*Loc. Cit., 28.*